Point of View

A Personal Response to Life, Literature and Politics

Point of View

A Personal Response to Life, Literature and Politics

Point of View

A Personal Response to Life, Literature and Politics

Nayantara Sahgal

PRESTIGE

Published by
Prestige Books
3/28, East Patel Nagar
New Delhi 110 008

ISBN: 81-7551-017-X

1997

Photo Typesetting by
Pivot Computers
Delhi 110 006
Ph. 2934490

Printed at
Mehra Offset Press
New Delhi 110 002

Contents

Addresses at Literary and Academic Conferences

Political Commentary 1969-74

Writings Connected with the Emergency 1975-77

A Miscellany

Introduction

A collection of my public addresses delivered at literary conferences was suggested to me by a friend, Ranjana Ash, who is a literature tutor, specializing in South Asian literature, at the University of London. To this I have added a selection of my published articles. The political pieces were chosen for the importance their subject matter had for public opinion, and for the country's future, when I wrote them; the others because they reflect some aspect of myself, in thought or in feeling.

Part one, "Of Myself and My Family," sets me down where I belong. Two articles in this section, written twenty-four years apart, pay tribute to the irrepressible spirit who was my mother, Vijaya Lakshmi Pandit. The last, "Friends, This is India," was commissioned by the *Guardian* in 1992 for a series in which writers around the world reflected on their nationality. It is included here for its portrait of the home I grew up in during the years of the struggle for freedom from British rule, and is reprinted with the *Guardian's* permission. The title "Commitment a Style" uses the word commitment in its proper meaning, as against the meaning it acquired during the 1970s when the government called for "committed" officials, academics and judges in place of the independent tradition and professional standards that had prevailed until then. This article, and "Turning Point," brought my unconventional personal life to my readers' notice long before India entered the permissive era. I considered the risk of exposure worth taking if it touched a responsive chord in those who mattered to me as the constant invisible presence in my life as a writer.

The public addresses in Part Two—the reason for this book—represent my most recent self, and contain the platform, philosophy and point of view that are integral to my approach.

Part Three contains the five political articles mentioned above, which mirror political developments during the early 1970s when the press and other free institutions were under attack from an increasingly autocratic establishment. In my intense foreboding that we were being marshalled toward some form of dictatorship I wrote as I did, not in the conceit that anything I wrote would make a difference, or deflect the tidal wave approaching us, but because times of crisis demand plain speaking.

Part Four consists of my reactions—two of them, letters—to the 19-month dictatorship of 1975-77 known as the Emergency. This section starts, however, with a presentation I made a year before the Emergency at a conference on Leadership in South Asia at the School of Oriental and African Studies, University of London, when I introduced my paper on Indira Gandhi's political style. Significantly, none of the learned professors present took my fears for India's democratic future seriously, but when events bore these out I expanded my paper into a book *Indira Gandhi: Her Road to Power*. After censorship brought the curtain down on free expression I had to resort to metaphor to express my concern for our lost liberties. "The Clear Call of Conscience" is an example. The last item in this section is the introduction I wrote to a collection of my speeches and writings during the Emergency published under the title *A Voice for Freedom*.

Part Five is a miscellany, chosen for its variety, written between 1966 and 1993. I then gave up the monthly column I was writing for the *Sunday Observer*. I had already stopped contributing political commentary to the *Indian Express*. As a freelance writer I have had a long and happy relationship through critical, and sometimes tumultuous times, with the press of my country, and the privilege of working with editors of courage and integrity. In the singularly unintelligent era now upon us, dominated by the "market," and fuelled by advertising and consumerism, it seems best to reserve comment until times change. As they will. They always do.

Of Myself and My Family

Equality with Tears*

I am not sure that my mother Vijaya Lakshmi Pandit, wanted to be anybody's equal. Married to a man** who was highly literate in several European and Indian languages besides his own Marathi, and a Sanskrit scholar of some reputation, she considered herself the least educated person she knew. It frequently upset her that she could not speak German and Italian, Bengali and Gujarati, and had no interest in learning Polish. And how did one make any kind of an impression on life, or contribute anything useful to it, when partnered by a man who did everything brilliantly? She decided to leave it all to him and spent the first few years of her married life having babies. But in 1930, her first baby-free year, she made an entry into public affairs through the Municipal Board at Allahabad.

This was not her own idea. She took the offer with qualms, nervous about her capacity to hold her own in discussions in a roomful of men, most of them much older than herself and all with considerable civic and political experience. There was no question of her refusing the opportunity. She had a husband and a brother who did not believe opportunities should be refused, and saw to it that she did no such thing. So she did the next best thing. She persuaded her husband and Lal Bahadur Shastri, both Board Members, to sit on either side of her at meetings, and thus reassured by the presence of two reliable and comfortingly familiar men she hesitantly ventured into the world beyond domesticity.

The U.P., though an amalgam of cultures, is heavily weighted by orthodoxy, both Muslim and Hindu. Its feudal traditions are not the kindest background for any young woman to try her mettle in the rough-house of politics. In 1936 home was still considered the proper place for a woman of breeding, and her election campaign that year became my mother's next big hurdle. Even coarse khaddar and the dust of her Kanpur constituency did not succeed in hiding the fact that she was an exceptionally beautiful woman, and much comment was made on the fact

---

* *The Sunday Standard*, 13 March 1966

** Ranjit Sitaram Pandit

that she wore sleeveless blouses, a novelty at the time. It was unseemly and immodest to campaign in sleeveless blouses,* calling attention to her arms,her critics said. My mother was inclined to be hurt and tearful about this attack, but my father's reply was that her arms would naturally attract attention since they were attractive. He advised her to pay no attention to the criticism and to go on campaigning.

In the course of the campaign her rival candidate brought a court case against her which would have been enough to phase a much more intrepid politician. She sent distress signals to her husband and her brother,** begging them to be present in court with her on the appointed day. Both men promptly wrote back from different parts of the U.P. that they were busy with their own election campaigns, and that they were convinced she was perfectly capable of appearing in court without their help. Deciding they were both useless in a crisis my mother next appealed to Govind Ballabh Pant, who answered gallantly that he would of course, come and lend her his moral support. Calmed by this reply and the knowledge of his stalwart presence she entered court to find her husband and brother present too. She told them afterwards that had she not been so grateful and delighted at their unexpected appearance, she would have treated them to the cold looks they deserved.

Pantji's offer of a Ministership in his Cabinet was her next opportunity and she faced it with some trepidation. How did one suddenly become a Minister and take on all sorts of new, unaccustomed responsibilities? And what about the home which till now had been in Allahabad, and the children for whom she would have little time? And how much time would she and her husband have together, if his work continued in Allahabad? But she became a Minister and went to Lucknow, and her husband divided his time between Allahabad and Lucknow, and their children grew, their lives nourished and filled by two vital, active parents. Any inconvenience occasioned by frequent separations was overcome by the solid and satisfying fact of worthwhile work being done and much fulfilment gained in the process. In order to prevent my mother's head being turned by her new importance her brother proceeded to refer to her as "Honourable Minister" or "Honourable One" and sometimes as "Ancient One." She was a youthful thirty-seven at the time.

Ministership between 1937 and 1939, when the Congress Ministries resigned on the issue of India's participation in Britain's war effort, was

---

* The Government of India Act, 1935, provided for elections in the eleven provinces of British India.

** Jawaharlal Nehru

an exhausting and exhilarating experience. It was a race against time to get as much constructive legislation pushed through as possible within a government framework that was neither sympathetic nor cooperative toward Congress policies. At any time the delicate balance between the Congress and the British government might be upset and the Ministries out of office. And it was exhilarating because a start was made at putting Congress programmes into effect. By and large there was a spirit of enthusiasm and the feeling of being involved in the making of history. For my mother it was her first paid job and she gained immensely in confidence as she earned her living and contributed to household expenses. There were periods of trial, as during the Budget session of the Legislature when intimidated by a sea of statistics she wrote to her Parliamentary Secretary: "These figures alarm me. Will P.S. kindly explain?" The reply came back immediately: "Figures alarm you? I cannot believe it. I know H.M. is prepared to face battalions and mould the destiny of nations. I can only take her note as an encouragement to me in my work." Nevertheless, he attached a note explaining the figures.

Those two years as India's first woman Cabinet Minister were the beginning, for my mother of an impressive series of firsts. In 1946 she was the first woman to lead a delegation to the United Nations. The following year she became the world's first woman ambassador, and a few years later the first and so far the only woman to be elected President of the United Nations General Assembly. And for an "uneducated" woman she collected a formidable number of honorary degrees from the world's most famous universities. It is obvious to us, her children, that though some people might be born equal, others have equality thrust upon them.

My New Novel: *The Day in Shadow**

One of the things this book is about is divorce. Som's is a hard, competitive, violent world and he thrives on it, while Simrit has been brought up with a different kind of awareness about what the world should be. Awareness—if you take that to mean the sensing of possibilities and sensitivity to what lies beyond your immediate insistent environment—is a kind of disease that grows with age. It makes you thinner-skinned as you grow older. The horny outer layers of conventional reaction, of your own safe place in the world, keep falling off, exposing more and more of the nerve beneath—and you begin to feel every current in your environment more keenly. If the currents don't rhyme with your inner make up the experience can become very painful. Even if you have been numb and content for years, enclosed in a comfortable formula of living, you eventually find out it won't do. Awareness breaks through—uninvited, relentless—and you have to look it in the face.

This is what happens to Simrit in *The Day in Shadow*. Her marriage to Som has worked quite well for years. It has all the hallmarks of success; mutual attraction, money, prospects, and a sexual relationship that flowers during her pregnancies. That is why she goes on having children. But there comes a time when all these ingredients of success become the instruments of her torture. What goes wrong? Another man in her life? A change in Som? Frighteningly enough, the growing realization that life is an intensely personal confrontation. The way you live has to agree with your mental makeup and your emotions, your liver and your glands, and even sex is finally tied up with all of these. Simrit discovers that "Sex was no more just sex than food was just food. . . . Once the edge was off hunger a meal had to be more than food. And once past its immediacy, sex had its visions too—of tenderness, of humour, of more than a physical act."

It would have been easier to explain Simrit's divorce in terms of another man. Only I am sure her kind of break was more paralyzing be-

* *The Hindustan Times*, 18 December 1971

cause it could not be explained so simply. Besides, lots of marriages survive adultery. It is a tension between couples, a way of life on which two people cannot agree, that becomes difficult to cope with.

Why write a novel about a divorce? Because writing of any sort helps to put your own world in order, all the shapeless, bewildering fragments of it. It helps you to figure out what is happening in and around you. And in this book I tried to figure out something that had happened to me—the shattering experience of divorce. There are things that will never be understood until they are written, and sometimes not even then. But writing helps the process. So Simrit turned out to be somewhat like me, even to being a writer, and very stupid about practical matters.

But I wanted to do more in this novel than convey this emotional holocaust and how it affects a woman. I wanted to show how even in a free country like ours where women are equal citizens, a woman can be criminally exploited without its creating a ripple. Again I am not speaking of any obvious, recognizable form of exploitation against which most people will naturally raise a cry. If a man beats his wife, for instance, hardly anyone will condone the fact. But if at divorce he inflicts a financial settlement on her that enslaves her with taxes and makes it impossible for her to make a decent living, no one will take any notice because this is the kind of beating where the blood and bruises don't show. But in addition—and this is the crux of the matter—nobody bothers about it even when they do. Simrit in this story finds she has to serve as a tax convenience for her ex-husband all her life, and that tied up in this way, she will never be able to make an adequate living for herself. An extraordinary state of affairs, yet nobody thinks so, neither the lawyer who drafted the settlement, nor the court that approved it, nor even Simrit herself when she signed it, womanlike, without understanding what it was all about. The worst part of it is that Simrit, like most women, can be casually exploited because she is so eminently exploitable. She is a passive creature to whom things happen. She is not part of the creating, acting world. Even when the enormity of the settlement is explained to her she cannot bring herself to believe it, much less to fight it. Divorce for woman-nature is almost a sin, and in expiation of her share of the guilt she stays mute and acquiescent over the settlement, willing to accept it as part of her Karma. Simrit is symbolic of the Hindu race.

The story takes place in Delhi and I can never think of Delhi without thinking of politics, Parliament, India. All these come into the book and form a big part of it. Everything around the writer is material for a novel, but few settings are as dramatic as Delhi today. I don't mean the present war situation but the general political atmosphere. I believe we move in a different medium today and that the Indian future is no longer geared, as it once was, to an Indian past. Raj, to whom Simrit turns for help, is a Member of Parliament, a man who believes in life, not Karma, and tries to persuade Simrit to do the same. He has a Herculean task because Simrit is not an individual—she is a culture, a tradition, a patient, enduring passivity. This is not Hinduism, but it is what Hinduism has come to represent.

And this is the theme underlying the novel, that Hinduism must change, revitalize itself if Hindus are to become an active, positive breed with something to give the world, and not be swept away by alien tides. It may not be fashionable to talk of religion or to be a believer, but I have never been in the least concerned about fashions or conformity. I am a believer in the greatest and most comprehensive metaphysics known to man—Hinduism—and in its powerful potential to provide men and women with a buoyant base for action. The question is—and no novel can answer it—will we discover it in time?

Some Recent Books

Since books became a high-powered industry there is such a glut of them that I do my best *not* to keep up with the written word. So I read very little, and very little at a time. I hoard new acquisitions like miser's gold and wait for work-free spells when I can really enjoy them. Sometimes I keep a book for months before I read it. I generally avoid thousand-page masterpieces because they are too big and bulky to relax with, and also because I am certain they would—like people—be healthier and happier if they weighed less. Maybe that's why I write with economy. There is so much in print, I feel every word I add to the mountain should count. I love fiction and read it for the same reasons that I write it: to refresh and companion myself, to learn more about myself and other people, to be enticed and involved and emotionally moved. My favourite fiction is the kind that either glitters or yearns. Two books that measured up in the past year were Angela Carter's collection of stories, *The Bloody Chamber*, and Amitav Ghosh's novel, *The Shadow Lines*. I don't know any other writer who lights up language and makes beautifully polished jewels of words the way Carter does. These are old fables and fairy tales retold, this time for grownups, with strange new twists and turns to Bluebeard, Puss-in-Boots and others, and no one can match her lovely rendering of the sensual and the sexual. Ghosh's novel is about Bengal (East and West) and London, and about the long close bond between two families. It has a dreamlike flow and sometimes confusion with houses and cities suddenly changing places, and characters suddenly growing up while two of them are sitting on a dusty floor under a dining table. It is also about frontiers, about love and obsession, and about all this being part of our subcontinent's divided haunted self, even perhaps the realization that our ghosts are not easily exorcised and that we must live with them. It was the kind of book that need a yearning reader, a role I effortlessly filled.

Commitment a Style*

When it came to actually doing it, I couldn't. Living together without marriage held too many terrors. It might be all right in some place off the beaten track, but definitely not in the full avid glare and publicity of Delhi. We** were not arty types, or brazen, or given to sensation. We were both rather quiet responsible citizens, myself with children. I quailed at the very thought and argued. I declared that until we could marry we would live apart.

He found a flat for me and the children and I moved in. I was righteous and unapologetic about going back on our earlier joint decision. One thing was certain, I repeated. No living together till we could marry. It had seemed possible and even simple earlier when we had planned it, but faced with it with the people next door, the people down the road, the people in his office, the people at parties, the people we knew and the ones we had yet to meet—it was unthinkable. Oh yes, I had *said* I would face it, but how could I? I wriggled out of our plan like a coward, or a liar, or a respectable person concerned with propriety and mindful of Other People. Between us lay my cowardice, limp and soggy, unattractive to look at. I ignored it. What mattered was Other People.

What else could I do? This was Delhi and everybody knew me and him. I'd rather die, I said, than be talked about. We knew Delhi well but this was the first time we had come to live in it. So we were newcomers in a sense, with a future to build, a living to earn—he as an official who, in the course of his career, had achieved the category of excellence and distinction, and something more: the capacity to influence and enliven those who worked with him, and a faithful circle of friends and admirers. He was not making much headway with me and his anger was directed more at my fears than at my mulish obstinacy, supported, he said, by an arrogant Brahmin tradition that could never, never bend, never admit it might be in the wrong. He was afraid too, but being afraid was not a good enough reason for not acting. And backsliding was un-

* *The Sunday Statesman*, 9 April 1972

** The author and E.N. Mangat Rai

forgivable. He was merciless about people who backed out.

But, I insisted, there was his career to consider. How many were there like him, and how could he jeopardize it all by stepping out of line? I knew he loved his work the way he loved all the big and little things he got involved with. He agreed a career was to be valued, and he valued his own. He had earned his reputation every inch of the way. No family with a capital F, no fortune, no connections had seen him through. It was his own creation, an involvement so fully and deeply experienced that it could be given up whole and without grief, given up gladly the way a child is when it is grown and you have done the best you could for it. And besides, he said, life was bigger than a career, bigger than advancement and promotion and paraphernalia. So if any of that suffered, it would be a pity but no tragedy.

"We could have lived in Dharwar," he reminded me, "and avoided Delhi altogether. There's a whole fascinating country to choose from."

He had passed through Dharwar on a train once and liked it. He preferred small places, and making a fresh start in a new place did not worry him. Doing what? Anything that did not mean a full-time job or making a lot of money. He refused to join the money chase. There were so many better things you could do with time.

"We could still go to Dharwar," he said.

Delhi had never been his cup of tea. He had consistently refused a Delhi posting—surely a phenomenon in the civil-service. I did not know anyone else who had. He hated the scramble for top-drawer jobs and power. India for him had always been the provinces, the countryside, the hills. There was the rest of the world to choose from, too, but this was home and neither of us wanted to go away for long. Finally, for convenience sake we had chosen Delhi.

"You see how impractical this is," he said, "I have to come to see you on a bicycle."

The bicycle, borrowed from a friend, stood below. I did not know anyone in Delhi's upper strata, or anywhere else, who rode a bicycle. It, along with the simplicity of his own move to Delhi, made me very conscious of all my possessions, back-breaking to pack and unpack. I began to think about the art of shedding. The bicycle became a poignant reminder of some essential simplicity I had lost during my own move to Delhi, of the courage I had mislaid along the way. It seemed to belong to a fresher time in our relationship, to a world where real things had mattered. It represented now the paradox of a man at the top of his career and devoted to it, but calmly indifferent to its prestige, its plums and its prizes. Man had not then reached the moon, but here, I thought, was one reaching for the stars—on a bicycle.

I would try reaching too. I packed my luggage and moved with the children to the house he had been allotted, and prepared to face the onslaught of Other People. We were not strangers to non-conformity but this, I thought, was going to be like hacking steps where no steps had ever been, in the cold rock face of a society unused to such situation. But though there was upheaval enough, involving ourselves, the storms of growing children and the adjustments to be made from past to present, Other People were not part of it. They unfolded along the way as a courteous and kindly breed, ready with interest, affection and help. Of one thing there was no sign—condemnation.

"Why should there be?" he said, "This is not the high fever of passing excitement and attraction, not part of any permissive wave. This is commitment, and people recognize it when they see it."

Three years later, when commitment became a fashionable word in official circles and he was found not committed enough to retain,* I could have wept for the setup that lost him. It did not really know the meaning of the word or the quality that inspired it. In 1971, as we moved out of the house where we had faced and shared adventure, I knew that in company with him I had learned that commitment was a state of grace in which nothing was impossible.

---

* E.N. Mangat Rai resigned as Special Secretary to The Ministry of Petroleum and Chemicals because he was convinced he could not, with self-respect, work under the government of the time.

The Testament of an Indo-Anglian Writer*

I am Indian—by blood, nationality, upbringing and conviction and Western by virtue of my English-medium education. Starting with the local convent in Allahabad, I went on to five years at an American school, Woodstock, at Mussoorie, followed after a gap by four years at Wellesley College in the United States. The change to Woodstock was due to Gandhiji's call to boycott British and Government-aided institutions, and the decision to send my elder sister and me to America was taken when my parents, then prisoners in Naini Jail, Allahabad, were told that their daughters would not be permitted entry to an Indian college unless they gave a guarantee not to take part in "political activities."

We were not, and never had been, people who gave guarantees that curtailed freedom. And the whole idea of taking a decision under duress-even had it not been demanded by a foreign government—was abhorrent to my parents. The alternative, of sending us away, was breathtakingly uncertain in its possibilities. The year was 1943 and the war was at its height. We would, if we went to America, have to travel by troop ship through dangerous waters. We would not be told our route or our port of arrival, and we would have to find our own way, at the tender ages of sixteen and nineteen respectively, in a strange country of which my parents had no personal knowledge and little in the way of contacts. Safety and security dictated that we stay at home and give whatever guarantee the Government required, and our anxious relatives advised strongly that we should. But men and women with the hunger for freedom in their souls seldom make important choices for reasons of safety. In our household the word was anathema. My father had tossed it overboard when he threw up a lucrative law practice to join the national movement. My mother's family tradition and set-up of wealth and abundance had similarly been voluntarily discarded when her father Motilal Nehru decided to follow Gandhi. She herself had had the greatest satisfaction in abandoning what women's Lib now calls the "stereotype"

* *Indian and Foreign Review*, 1 December 1972

woman image and setting out to succeed and sparkle in a hitherto masculine field—politics. As far as these two were concerned, torpedoes on the high seas and an unknown future were hazards they would far rather subject their young daughters to than any humiliating curtailment of self-respect, safe though it might be.

I have gone into this at some length because their attitude typified the general aspiration of Gandhi's India. I don't believe my parents were unusual in courage, but they had unusual opportunity, above all the opportunity of trying and testing their values in the daily grind of the national movement, of constantly having to put their beliefs to work. This kept their sensibilities sharp and their choices crystal clear. There was no muddy compromise, nor, for that matter, the grim joyless atmosphere of self-righteousness. There was laughter in and around my parents and a gaiety that seemed to enhance their good looks and vivid personalities. Their outlook was refreshingly open, partly the result of their own education, travel and knowledge of the world. We were Indian, and supremely aware of it, but in this Indian home we learned that freedom, justice and aesthetics had no frontiers. Beauty, achievement, and all the lessons of history belonged to mankind. The one-world theme, so characteristic of civilized Indian thinking, was another dominant strain throughout the struggle for independence. "Where the world has not been broken up into fragments by narrow domestic walls," Rabindranath Tagore had written, "Into that heaven of freedom, my Father, let my country awake." "I do not want my house to be walled in on all sides and my windows to be stuffed," wrote Gandhi, "I want the culture of all lands to be blown about my house as freely as possible." These and others—Vivekananda, Radhakrishnan, Sarojini Naidu—had, in their consciousness of the universal, represented much more than India, and in doing so had become part of the world's consciousness of India.

No narrow frontiers, then, for us. They would have been impossible anyway, living as we did with my uncle, Jawaharlal. He brought the world to our doorstep, right into our thoughts and emotions, moving us to anger and tears when he spoke of fascism and the evils it perpetrated in Abyssinia, in Spain and among its own people. Yet with all this he gave us the accompanying certainty that it was a wonderful world, despite crisis, and that its gifts and riches were within the reach of the inquiring mind.

We went to America, our first experience of a free country, and for the first time we realized what it was like to live in one. In America, freedom—unlike in England, where a sophisticated and mature people, grown old in it, took it for granted—was still heady and intoxicating, like wine or a brand new, vibrant idea. People were ardent about it. "This is a free country" was a joking rejoinder to remarks about whether one should make this or that choice, yet it was earnestly meant. Freedom was a cherished possession, belligerently defended. In India it had been haunting in its lack, a distant star on the horizon, something to work and ache for, often at stupendous personal cost. In America it was in one's lap, on one's tongue, where, I suddenly discovered, it belonged. It was one's very own.

It was a fatal encounter that entered into my very bones. The need for freedom, I knew once and for all, went far beyond political or economic definition. It no longer applied only to a country. From the depths of everything my parents had taught me and demonstrated through the way they lived and worked, it became a solid value. I knew that never in any circumstances, personal or national, whether in my capacity as student, or later as wife, mother or citizen, would I let it go. The freedom to think, to write, to *be*, was what life was all about. All of this I thought about and wrote down in diaries and in letters home—in English.

I was a lover of language, not any particular one but all those I had been exposed to. I enjoyed the sound and meaning of words, what one could accomplish by using and arranging them. Words were the stuff of magic, and there was the thrill of expression when facility came one's way. I had felt this with Hindi, studied with a pandit at home and later as a subject for matriculation from high school. The prose I read did not touch any chord in me, but the poetry was enchantment, from the Tulsidas Ramayana to the modern poets, and I remember with what fascination I listened to Bachchan's recitation of his *Madhushala* at Anand Bhawan, our home, during the days of my cousin Indira's marriage. I could quote extensively from the Hindi poets and took pride in my growing vocabulary. The family spoke Hindustani, with a leaning toward Urdu, and my elders humoured me by sending for me when the correct Hindi word was required.

I shared my excitement over Hindi with my father, a considerable linguist, whose mother tongue was Marathi, and chosen field of study, Sanskrit. Some day he was going to teach me his beloved Sanskrit, but with all the strenuous demands on his time and his tragically early death as the result of an illness in prison, the day never came. When I got back from college in America, my distinguished aunt, Pandita Kshama Rao, offered to teach me Sanskrit by the "direct method," which she assured me produced quick results, but by then I was involved with a young man and thoughts of marriage, and I gave the direct method the go-by.

In college I had made the acquaintance of two more languages,

Spanish and Russian, studying the latter with Vladimir Nabokov, who later became famous as the author of the best-selling *Lolita*. Mr. Nabokov, handsome and cultured, was in love with two languages, his own and English, and his enthusiasm was contagious. For a start he wrote the word "kneega" (book) on the blackboard and made us repeat it several times. "Do you like it? Is it pleasing to you?" We did not proceed until we had thoroughly savoured the music of "kneega."

But language was a complex thing. To one who needed to write—as ·exploration and release—relationship with it became much more than utilitarian. Language had to get under one's skin. Conversational fluency in the classroom or at a dinner party was one thing and long-term, sustained expression quite another. I did not take the conscious decision, when I began to write for a living, that English would be my medium. It happened that way because I had the reading and reference for it over a large number of years. It was most natural for me to write in English. I thought that some time I would write in Hindi, too, but I had not reckoned then with time or with the urges and pressures of style. Language may come easily. Style does not. It has to be worked for, given the sun, wind and dew of the current scene in its literature and ideas. Style does not come ready-made. It develops. It has to be nurtured and polished, and it is finally what distinguishes the professional from the amateur, the disciplined from the casual. In literature and art, perhaps even in science, style is shape and structure built by the skilled use of tools. It has, ultimately, a lot to do with restraint. Even a florid style obeys rules. In any walk of life a sense of style sets apart the engineer, the artisan, the administrator, from his counterpart who merely does a pedestrian job. Anywhere, the worker spends his time learning the mastery of his tools, learning how to be simple, how to create without waste. In writing, except in unusual cases (of which Nahokov is one), life is not long enough to achieve this process in more than one language. A man will speak several languages with ease. He will seldom write as well in two.

So I continued as I had begun, in English, sharing my pleasure in it with three generations before me who had hated English rule but loved English things, and had found it perfectly possible to differentiate between the two. Because of this, when freedom came, it was enough to break with British rule. We did not have to destroy the institutions or the language we had inherited as a result of that rule. No loss of pride was involved in keeping what was useful and worthwhile. There are those who like destruction for its own sake, or need it as a manifestation of patriotism and a proof of national honour, but they did not have their way. Commonsense prevailed.

The attitude is not quite the same today, of course. English, like so much else that has served us well and truly during twenty-five years of freedom, is coming under fire. Oddly enough, those who want to wipe it out, apart from being fancifully impractical people, do not realize they want to eradicate more than a British inheritance. They want to root out something uniquely Indian, uniquely part of us through our history: the capacity to contain paradoxes and even enjoy them. There has never, until today, been a fierce either-or mentality in this country, never the need to murder one idea, or possibility, or loyalty to make room for another. In India even opposites have been able to thrive, and their doing so has never involved any compromise of Indian integrity. It was this fluidity, this flexibility that made us capable of change without violence. Are we still capable of it?

Besides, if English is not an Indian language today, is Urdu also foreign? How far back must an institution or an influence date before we can call it our own? And how shall we ever separate the thousand strands woven into our fabric through the British connection, when even a village band in the heart of the Punjab or Uttar Pradesh countryside accompanies a rural bridegroom with a Scottish tune, or something very like it? It is time to re-affirm good sense about English—an important world language we are fortunate enough to know—and to realize that great writing from India will emerge, not from any particular language, but from men and women imaginatively and emotionally identified with India, who will be able to portray the Indian realities.

Turning Point*

Turning points are not always obvious or dramatic. One may not even begin to realize till years later that a particular event or decision marked a turning point in one's life. Marriage, a routine enough occurrence, was the first one in mine. It closed the doors on the kind of life I had known and the person I had been until then. Briefly, this life and person could, I suppose, be summed up as partaking of freedom. I grew up in an India that was not free. But all around me at home, freedom—personal, political, spiritual—was a prime value, a necessity. No breath of authoritarianism ever touched my growing years. I was conscious of being continually stretched in mind and spirit, of being encouraged to be venturesome, of doing the daring rather than the timid thing, of taking risks rather than playing safe, and I was keenly aware of the joy of being myself, like every other person a unique human being.

I went to college in America and in a sense during those four years I never left home. I took it all with me, the loves, the loyalties, the way of life I had known, I found that they grew and blossomed and found new ways of expressing themselves in what was, for the first time in my experience, a free country. Then it was time to come home, and I was up against the unwritten law of most societies—the American as much as our own—that it was time to marry. I have often wondered since at the lifelong damage this stern and implacable expectation inflicts on the young and sensitive, especially those young women who have just begun to spread their wings and not had time to discover even a fraction of themselves. The clamps descend, the whole future is poured into a mould, and the first faint stirrings of selfhood are sacrificed to the rigorous demands of marriage and motherhood, sacrified often forever. The possibilities and achievements a society loses in this process must involve one of the most deliberate exercises in human waste imanigable. I was fresh and full of philosophy, history and art, full of confidence in myself, one part of my mind groping for what I would do next. But another part of me was heavily overlaid by the duty I must per-

* *Femina*, 1976

form—marriage. The false answer we are given to our doubts at such a time is that every girl must "settle down." She can do what she has to do after she marries. She cannot, of course. Not for many years. Perhaps never, for eventually there may be very little of her, and of life, left to do it with.

Marriage unsettled me disastrously. For the first time I came across the shocking assumption of inequality. A man's ego and ambition, I learned, must be served first. In case of conflict, the man's will and desires must prevail. Eager not to be found wanting I became docile and obedient, a "good wife." Soon I had children and in between looking after them I wrote three books. I was uneasy and restless adjusting to the demands of a personality and an environment whose goals and texture were different from anything I had known or been comfortable with. But if I had any hankerings, I suppressed them. I rigidly ignored the feeling that I was in a room two feet square with no opening but a tiny grating high up in one wall. I tried not to look up at it. Out there somewhere was sunlight, and at night a forest of stars, but they were not for me. I was here in my two-feet-square room of my own choice. Nobody had forced me into it and I had no one else to blame.

By traditional standards I should have been "happy." I had every comfort, and provided I did as I was told, every kindness. In the mirror I looked glossy and pampered. What was missing was something as vital and essential to me as oxygen—an atmosphere of aspiration. My sickness went deep and every now and again it surfaced and made trouble, for its clamouring core was the inescapable truth that once you have lived in freedom, been truly yourself, you can never settle for less. You cannot take over a disguise, however decorative, for the rest of your days. You cannot pretend other values, another outlook on life. You can't honestly serve what you don't believe in.

There are people who when they realize they have walked into a dead end, turn around and walk away from it. Gaugin apparently did. I have friends who have made breaks and difficult new beginnings. I became aware of my problem but not what I could do about it. I tried instead to adapt. Years later I made a Danish character in my novel *This Time of Morning* say: "We have every material thing we want. And sometimes it has dire effects. Like internal haemorrhage, when you don't know what has hit you but you're dying." And still later two of my heroines reflected something of my malaise. Saroj in *Storm in Chandigarh* looks out of her window: "A thin young moon hung in the sky, unimaginable distances from her, and tears filled her eyes for all of life that would not be denied." Simrit in *The Day in Shadow*, reduced to illness, "in a grief too continuous to be catered to," because she finds her husband's world of wealth and ambition devoid of the personal touch, longs for "a world whose texture is kindly. . . . Surely there is such a world." Even sex with her husband becomes a problem because she can no longer identify with his goals, and sex cannot be kept in a compartment by itself. These were pieces of me going into the men and women I created when I really began to write. But before that happened I went to Kashmir alone to finish work on a book.

The house I stayed in was bare according to my standards. My host, a recent friend, was busy with his tasks as Chief Secretary in the State. But there were huge chinars in the unkempt garden and something else—the fresh air of ideas, talk that took you to the ends of the earth and beyond, the reality of communication when there is real exchange between people, the re-discovery of equality and comradeship. For I had not come upon anything new. I had a feeling of homecoming. What I had not been able to do in fifteen years, I did in a few minutes. I settled down. I woke and slept and worked as if it were childhood and early morning again, and all of life innocent and waiting to be discovered. What followed for me was not an affair but a revolution, I knew that I had to live and create with the truth of my whole being, and unless I was allowed to do that within my marriage, I would have to face the ordeal of being thrown out of it. I was.

My second turning point came when, for reasons beyond my control, I had to make a decision to live with this man without marriage. I think now of the splendor of Muriel Rukeyser's lines:

> Escape the birthplace
> Walk into the world
> Refusing to be either slave or slaveholder.

At the time there were no heroics involved. There was a living to be earned and it meant hard work. I felt an enormous inner strength. In four years I wrote two novels and a textbook on the freedom movement for our schools, and established myself as a political columnist. Life became crowded with the problems of my growing children, and the torn-flesh feeling of divorce never left me. I am essentially a person who needs a great deal of solitude. I did not get it. I had to face the world continually at many levels, without the security of the married relationship or the cushion of money. And finally I stepped out, too, from the powerful supports of "family" and "background," and became, very simply, myself. My second turning point taught me many things, but one above all: I knew I would never be afraid of anything again as long as I lived. It takes half of life to achieve personhood but perhaps there is no greater glory.

The Virtuous Woman*

My great-grandmother became a *sati*. Somewhere in Bambuli village on the coast of Ratnagiri there may still be a shrine to her. I remember being told this when I was a child and it made the kind of impression on me that reading about *jauhar* in Rajput annals had done, when queens and their retinues of hundreds had died in flames. It was something distant, a terrifying, thrilling spectacle connected with "virtue" (female) and "honour" (male). It was a blend of history-culture-religion wrapped in the sanctified, impenetrable dust that shrouds an artificially preserved, rather than a living, heritage. It was romance. What I never could connect it with was reality, though real enough women had done these things.

I didn't hear, nor did I ask, why my great-grandmother had done this. And the event lay dormant in my consciousness for years until the 1970s brought the Emergency, which gave me an anguished awareness of the freedoms we had taken so much for granted and so suddenly lost. For not until I lost mine did I realize that most of my fellow citizens, especially women, had never been able to exercise theirs, or indeed known they had any to lose. The Emergency gave birth to a movement for civil liberties, and newspapers afterwards began to report their terrible abuses and violations in towns as well as rural areas. We read that in 1975, in Delhi alone, some three hundred women were burned alive by greedy in-laws. It was then that my burned Maharashtrian ancestress became a woman of flesh and blood and began to haunt me, and finally appeared in the next novel I wrote, *Rich Like Us*. She who belonged to one of the most independent traditions to which Indian women are heir, she who had never known purdah or the forms of serfdom the north imposes on its women, could she have gone to the pyre of her own free will? Was she drugged, dragged, forced? Did she really prefer death to life? And if so, is this the gruesome death anyone would choose when there are quicker ways of dying? But then, of course, *sati* is not only an awesome ending to a life. It is a human sacrifice, and sacrifice entails

* *The Tribune*, 24 December 1988

ceremonial, spectacle, witnesses. And if it is by free will, that will is the result of conditioning since the cradle, in a scenario where male "honour" and female "virtue" are a cult ferocious in its connotations and merciless in its demands.

Staying alive as a widow constituted an offence against these, leaving home constituted another, even in circumstances where home means humiliation, persecution, injury, and ultimately death, as with the three hundred burned brides in Delhi, and countless unregistered cases. For though the *sati* revival has been alarming enough to attract stringent new legislation, the commandment never to leave home is still absolute. And staying put is the *sati* equivalent humbly accepted by women in the tragic belief that there is no other choice. Female conditioning says you may on no account leave, that you may be thrown out. Tough luck.

I began, through the writing process, to unlearn all I had been taught, including that overpowering mix called history-culture-religion, and to discover who I was through the words I put on a page. While I was struggling with problems of personal emancipation, my fictional Rashmi, in *This Time of Morning*, achieved hers, leaving a marriage that had become an emotional wasteland. I was still struggling when Saroj in *Storm in Chandigarh* left her jealous, unreasonable, unfaithful husband, though she had two children and was heavily pregnant with her third. Of course, she took them with her. And by the time I had become a walk-out/ thrown-out combine, Simrit in *The Day in Shadow* had become one too, only with a whole horde of children—a number I left unspecified as against my three—showing that even this could be done. Later, Devi in *A Situation in New Delhi* and Sonali in *Rich Like Us*, close to live their achieving lives, independent of men.

But the stereotype rules most women's lives. The TV Ramayana and Mahabharata have done nothing to dispel it, and a good deal to refurbish it. They have stimulated no debate about why Rama who threw out his beloved wife is the example of perfect manhood, or why Gandhari who was moronic enough to keep her eyes bandaged because her husband was blind, is considered an ideal woman. Yet in the west, each new production of Greek tragedy interprets it afresh, each new Hamlet represents a contemporary quandary, and recently Lear became a Japanese. Even Jesus Christ is for any artist to interpret as he pleases, and faith is not defiled, nor Christianity reviled, if he is pictured as a human being with human desires. Why must Hinduism be kept in cotton wool? A unique opportunity has been lost in not re-telling our epics with lessons for our times. The same old dust envelops them, and a re-indoctrinated public stays drugged and docile while monstrous new temples are built to celebrate new *satis*, and riots break out the alleged birthplace of Rama.

It is clear the epics can only be re-examined when women take charge of their lives, when they dissect the stories of the female sacrificial examples they have been taught to worship, and ask: Could she have done this of her own free will? And if so, what manner of horrifying social pressures created such a will? Through the re-writing women do, new Sitas and Savitris will arise, stripped of false sanctity and crowned with the human virtue of courage. Then at last we will know why they did what they did, and how their lone, remote struggles can help our search for identity and emancipation.

Reflections on a Death in the Family*

Vijaya Lakshmi Pandit resigned her Lok Sabha seat in 1968, saying she felt out of tune with the politics of the time. Had she not moved out of political life then she may have had a difficult decision to make the following year when Mrs. Gandhi broke with the Congress to create a party in her own image, and later in her own name. Vijaya Lakshmi was deeply devoted to "family" as idea and as entity, and the Indian National Congress was in a sense as much her family as the one she was born into. The two were closely connected in her emotions and imagination, and the schism brought about in both by Mrs. Gandhi troubled her. Her own association with both had been lifelong. She had grown up in the Indian National Congress, entered local politics in Allahabad, was twice elected to the U.P. legislature, and twice to Parliament as a member of it. Under a Congress government she represented India at the United Nations, served as ambassador to the Soviet Union, the United States and Britain, and was governor of Maharashtra, all these with her brother and mentor as the country's leader.

During her long retirement in Dehra Dun, in isolation (until recently) both from the power structure and the family at Delhi, she wondered what the party of her childhood, youth and middle age had accomplished by tearing itself apart. Had policies been better served by the split? Had social and economic reform been advanced? Had the cause of women, or human rights received an impetus? What cause in fact could not have been better served by a united party built on the contribution of unknown men and women during the days when martyrdom was a freedom fighter's greatest reward, rather than one converted into a personal and dynastic vehicle? She did not believe dynasty could ever be the basis of a healthy democratic tradition. The fracture of political parties in recent years, with a leader's initial attached to every new split, has indeed made a farce of multi-party democracy, with the Indian scene representing a host of little egos and identities lobbying for

* *The Times of India*, 16 December 1990

themselves, instead of political parties united by their concern for India. When, in 1975, Vijaya Lakshmi overcame her reluctance to comment on the current scene, it was to protest against the suppression of civil liberties during the Emergency, and its open sanction to dynasty.

Her resignation in 1968 cost her more than her place in the political sun. It closed the door to family, which distressed her far more. A family, to her way of thinking, was a reason to get together for a cup of tea, a meal or a chat, to laugh or cry together in celebration or in sorrow. This did not happen once she left Delhi, for Pandit Nehru and Mrs. Gandhi had little in common temperamentally. I described the difference in a study of Mrs. Gandhi's political style: "Nehru's temperament was the fireside at which many warmed their hands, took strength, and went on their way to personhood, more confident for the encounter with him. Indira's was the flame—lone, dependent on shelter for its glow and survival, leaving its surroundings dark. . . . Nehru, effortlessly a leader of men, had the self-confidence of which equal relationships, personal and political, are born. Indira clung to 'family' as anchor, making it a platform for superiority. The era that dawned after 1969 was a black-and- white, either-or one. The camaraderie among political opponents, the team spirit in the Congress itself, the political differences and arguments that could co-exist along with family loyalty, and had done so throughout the struggle for freedom when Nehru and some of his close relatives were on opposite sides of the political fence, froze in their tracks. There was no room any more for the hurly-burly of opinions, or the free and civilized exchange of differences that had flourished in the sprawling family that both the Congress and the Nehrus had once been.

It is a mark of Vijaya Lakshmi's early, joint family upbringing, and the family atmosphere characteristic of that Indian home in spite of its western influences, that she remained part of the original joint family, never thought of herself as anything else, and continued to hope for the open door, the cup of tea, and a glimpse of the children being born and growing up. If she had one grief during retirement it was the fact that her brother's great-grandchildren, whom she considered her own, were strangers to her. On her part she made it clear when she campaigned for the Janata Party during the 1977 election that her campaign was political, not personal, and she would not go into her niece's constituency. I have never seen her so stricken and shocked as at Mrs. Gandhi's defeat in her constituency. Vijaya Lakshmi had never dreamed this might happen, though she had hoped the country would reject a government that had sanctioned a dictatorship.

Does India reward its achievers? What would have been more fitting than that she should have been made President after the Janata victory in 1977? Her prestige in India and abroad, her political and diplomatic experience gave her high qualifications for a post she would have adorned. The Janata party punished itself and perhaps deserved what it got when it elevated a man to the presidency who is widely believed to have betrayed his office and plunged the country into a midterm election it need never have had, which thereafter paved the way for dynasty.

Rajiv Gandhi's appointment as Prime Minister did not heal divisions in the country, but it opened the family door and mended a family breach. The affection, respect, and unfailing concern he showed toward the woman, by then in her eighties, whom he called his grandmother, made an enormous difference to her last few years. Visits and bonds were resumed. Help was at hand, jokes were shared, homilies delivered, criticism aired and no offence taken. She wanted her family under her roof for her ninetieth birthday and they immediately responded to her invitation, regardless of their political differences, travelling to Dehra Dun from Delhi, Lucknow and Kasauli for lunch on August 18th. It was a grand, and as it happened, farewell gesture to a woman who had always been passionately devoted to her family. All that remained was for Rajiv to arrange and personally supervise her last rites two and a half months later. This he did, with love and grace, and in a manner she would have considered befitting a member of her family. "I've lived too long," she often said, "No one should mourn me." So together we celebrated her life instead.

Vijaya Lakshmi Pandit did India proud. I am not sure if India did as well by her.

Friends, This is India—Hold on!*

The family belonged to the bourgeoisie spawned by British rule. Wealth and stability don't make for a life at the barricades so drama must have been their fate. It started with my grandfather, Motilal Nehru, whose early success at the Allahabad Bar enabled him in 1900 to buy a mansion in spacious grounds, engage an English-Irish tutor recommended by Annie Besant to prepare his son, Jawaharlal, for Harrow, and later an English governess for his daughters. He didn't send his laundry to Paris as rumoured, but he did invite all the children at his hotel in Baden-Baden to his daughter's fifth birthday party. His hospitality was famous and the patriarchal pride and bounty he lavished on his extended family were princely even by the standards of this hallowed Indian institution.

He loved a fight, from a wrestling bout to intellectual combat, and was mildly contemptuous of the elite assembly known as the Indian National Congress that met once a year at sessions festooned with oratory to petition the sovereign power for greater Indian participation in India's civil and military services, and elbow room for Indian capital in an economy run for British profit. Mainstream politics went no further and Motilal Nehru found it a tame substitute for action.

A fierier patriotism had sent a string of Indian revolutionaries to the gallows, life imprisonment, death in prison, or agitation abroad. National consciousness smarted under an imperial language of insult and exclusion—"the subject races" of officialese, the Gunga Din image, and white superiority so secure it did not need the prop of apartheid, but railway carriages, station retiring rooms, clubs and park benches reserved For Europeans Only testified to *herrenvolk* and master race.

The lawyers, professors and entrepreneurs of the Congress, however, depended on their dignified petitions to bring out the best in the British. They profoundly believed this buried "best" would arise and respond, granting India, like the white dominions, self-government and equal status in the empire. Trustfully they rallied to the empire's sup-

* *Guardian*, 5 March 1992

port in Europe's Great War and Gandhi, called Mahatma for the non-violent campaigns he had led in South Africa, himself recruited men for it.

It was after the war, when arbitrary arrest and jail without trial to ensure business as usual were followed on April 13, 1929, by the slaughter at Jallianwala Bagh, a walled garden in Amritsar where General Dyer's troops opened fire without warning on a crowd of thousands celebrating the spring festival, that the national agenda abruptly changed and Gandhi outlined his non-violent strategy for independence. Those who found civil disobedience too daunting or bizarre moved away from the action. Others, including the family, plunged into it.

Here it was that national and family history met, not quite as they must have in many families whose father, son or second cousin joined the fray, loyally supported by those who stayed outside it. In mine the household, jointly in thrall to a country whose destiny it took to be its own, jointly ended its old life and started its new one. A decade later the connection was rooted, permanent, mysterious. It gave their "we" and "ours" a curious breadth and span, considering they couldn't possibly have known they and theirs would in time rule India for close to 40 years.

The ABC of their total transformation was traceable. Point four of Gandhi's strategy called on lawyers to give up their practice. Father, son and son-in-law complied. Point nine required men and women "to make as much sacrifice as possible." They made a blazing bonfire of their British goods, donated the mansion to the party and moved into a small (by Motilal's patriarchal standards) domed house they built on the same estate. Both houses flew the Congress flag: saffron (for Hinduism) and green (for Islam), divided by a spinning wheel (for cottage industry) on a white (for unity) middle band. Point 10 about avoiding abuse as well as violence must have been more of a hurdle since the patriarch had a roaring temper when roused.

He had not reached the heights of his profession by suffering fools gladly or doing as he was told. But those must have been days when lions lay down with lambs, lords and vassals joined forces, worms turned. From infancy on I understood that the family with like-minded others all over the country had fallen into the radical regime of setting up committees in towns and villages, organizing these for political action, wearing and spinning the handspun cloth known as *khadi*, controlling their tempers, breaking laws and going to jail.

But if so many others were doing all this, then why had "destiny" struck only us? To be sure it had. I knew I was living in an Age, but which Age was another matter, with all time ever present around us. It was clear enough to our gardener for whom the family's move from the mansion to the domed house was the *Ramayana* all over again, just like Ram and Sita's halt the other day at the Bharadwaja ashram across the road on their journey into exile after renouncing the throne of Ayodhya.

Renouncing a property and a livelihood, not knowing what tomorrow would bring, had a high altitude effect on their personalities. My uncle Jawaharlal elatedly recalled a truncheon battering mounted police had given him during a demonstration against the Simon Commission in 1928.

The sacrificial role had not appealed to the patriarch who had dealt with it characteristically:

> I have nothing to say to your return to wine drinking, if you have (an injured mahatma had written to him on July 3, 1924) but if the report is to be relied on, I cannot but be grieved that you . . . should publicly drink and, what is worst, chaff at teetotalism.
>
> The statement, as reported, is too silly even for an after-dinner speech (Motilal Nehru replied). There were many good Muslims at this dinner who drank nothing but pure water. They heartily applauded my remarks and never for a moment dreamt that I was chaffing at teetotalism. . . . I must express my utter inability to understand how you can possibly reconcile yourself to the suggestion that I might drink privately if at all. I had . . . fully made up my mind to revert to total abstinence before the "prohibition" resolution was moved in the Assembly. But I am going to do nothing of the kind now. I simply cannot bring myself to yield to the puritanism affected in Congress circles . . . if there are idiots in the world who still think that, after all I have gone through during the last four years and am going through now, I can be capable of selling my soul to the devil for party purposes, let them think what they like.

The household I remember consisted of grandmother (beaten up herself in a demonstration), great aunt (the only saint of my acquaintance), the three I thought of as my parents—Ranjit and Vijaya Lakshmi Pandit and Jawaharlal Nehru—besides we three children, cousin Indira being a student in England until she came home to marry in 1942.

There was no mistaking the euphoria. The parents were beautifully, jubilantly in bloom. Jail conditions and the countryside's lung-choking dust played havoc with their health but made for high spirits. I've searched since—it being the fashion—for neurosis, some fearsomely sinister state of mind they might have been hiding, but have come back to the strangeness of their sanity instead. As I bruised my nose on *khadi* handkerchiefs, sweated over lessons on icebergs, the uses of whale blubber and other features of life on the North Pole, I must have realized the aura they radiated was happiness, and that the world would never be so innocent again.

The cosmopolitan life-style, vastly scaled down in a house stripped of extras, continued. The family saw themselves as people of their times and the times had always been complex beside this stretch of the Ganges. In the heartland of Hinduism, among the monuments and gardens of Islam, educated as the patriarch had been in Arabic and Persian, his son at Trinity, his son-in-law at Heidelberg, residents of a city whose roads were named after Englishmen, yet was a nerve centre of the national movement, they did not expect to be simple. My father, Ranjit Pandit, who had translated Kalhana's 12th century Sanskrit history of Kashmir, *Rajtarangini*, into English, sang "I want to cling to Ah ha hivy, if Ivy will cling to me" when he shaved. And a custom continued from the splendid days was the governesses. Someone younger than grandmother and great aunt had to be with us during parental absences. As Indian women did not enter the profession—though one Christian and one Hindu were found for brief periods—they were foreign.

What on earth were these sometimes bewildered white women of the 1930s and 40s doing (and why?) in an Indian family dedicatedly organizing revolt or biding their time in jail until they could? What did they make of such reminders to children as "We mustn't let the police see us cry," or letters from jail and elsewhere tenderly exhorting: "Non-violence is good, my darling. This wise talk about not causing injury, not retaliating, not giving blow for blow is very ancient talk in our country" (*letter to the author from Ranjit Pandit, July 1, 1940*). Or "Prepare yourself to play your part, with a strong body, a sensitive mind that is keen as the edge of a sword and a character that is wedded to high ideals" (*letter to the author from Jawaharlal Nehru, November 24, 1942*). Whatever their perplexities, they were amazingly at home in the domed house.

Mrs. Collins's melancholy repetition of "I love my husband and my husband loves me" became my first whole English sentence, and convinced grandmother that her husband had deserted her. Mrs. Belcher had a heavy smoker's yellow teeth and fingers. Her other addictions were strong tea and superstition. She had me slavishly uncrossing knives, quailing at number 13 and cowering at her story of the voice from the English cemetery croaking, "I want my buttered toast." The parents having discarded the shadowy citadel in which part of every Indian lives, regretfully replaced her with a Swiss. But Mademoiselle Colin was eased out when they found us carolling "Bel fascismo e no salvesta" from the anthem to Il Duce. Miss Ornsholt introduced us to the Viking saga and her side interest, the levitating lamas of Tibet. And when Miss Mills took leave to get her second abortion it was considered prudent not to let her return though her readings out loud from Wilde and Shaw had been scintillating. Miss Mills, pointing to a picture in the library, of my uncle in his Harrow Rifle Corps uniform, had enlightened a visitor, "Oh, that's Pandit Nehru when he was in the British army." Mrs Chew, a Chinese refugee from Singapore, smoked bhang with my best friend's brother to console herself in her exile.

I Hail Maryed at one school, sang Yes, Jesus Loves Me at another, aware that these, like the heroism of Clive and the villainy of the natives, were neither here nor there in the huger, older universe I inhabited at home. Of this my father taught me on walks under the stars, the coolest time to venture out during blistering summers, so that authentic history including the parents were living and theirs had been witness to, was ineluctably linked to the galaxies. I seemed always to be looking up, gazing at their positions in the sky and learning their names along with historic landmarks in the struggle for freedom here on earth.

The Bible gave me no trouble. Its illustrated Jehovah sailed so wrathful and magnificent on clouds high up above the hapless humans huddling below, he could have been grandfather, and uncle the compassionate Christ. Crucifixion and resurrection? They, my father said, were the meaning of what was happening up and down this land. On religion proper I consulted great aunt and had it from her that Krishna Bhagvan, playing bewitchingly on his flute, or the grand Shiva in tigerskin and ashes, appeared before the true devotee to grant his dearest wish. Mine, just in case, was: Kick out the King. The vision would vanish, my eyes would fly open, and the King would be gone from our stamps. The parents had no such familiarity with the Almighty. Since the patriarch's refusal to perform a purification ceremony on his return from his first voyage overseas, the family had been ostracized by the orthodox. This caused much handed-down hilarity, as did Indians who prospered by British grace and favour, and the pity of the orthodox for us poor children, no dowry, who'd marry us? When the Viceroy asked the public to pray for the British empire and victory against Hitler, my father wrote:

> I was rather far from the Viceroy and was pretty sure he would not notice if I did not pray for the British empire, nor did I know if

> God existed. If he does exist, we may be sure he knows what to do with it *[letter from Ranjit Pandit, May 24, 1940]*.

The Viceroy's God was in any case tainted by the imperial connection, a deity "beneath whose awful hand we hold/Dominion over palm and pine," and his appeal a choice piece of irony when he hadn't minded Hitler's rise. The only Providence the family believed in was one that had ordained India to nurture a staggering variety of humanity, and carve out of it a symphony of differences which the world had not yet labelled "nation." The national movement, embracing regions, religions, languages, and every racial strain and colour of the human race, was this identity in essence, the mosaic that would constitute nationality.

The parents expected nationalism to disappear when freedom and nationality were ours, as they were sure it must eventually from the face of the earth, for it was not the mystic, inarticulate snarl of blood and gut that Europeans had made it to explain their ferocious tribal wars, or the God-and-Mammon duo of their expansion abroad. Asian sovereignties had never had this dimension of fantasy. A civilized world's borders would be porous, its nations would be geographical, not militant, expressions. After all, when had ordinary people worried about frontiers? Their cattle wandered across them. They loved their fields, streams and forests, and prayed to village gods. Their ultimate national experience was one of being shackled to the same level of primitive subsistence, under a burden of land revenue and debt. Gaining Indian nationality was less about politics, or power (too distant) than about reorganizing society. While every resonant sentence the parents spoke or wrote deconstructed empire—which they never doubted would vanish like a pimple off a face—it recreated India a republic of equals, one they themselves might not all live to see. One of them did not, my father contracting pleurisy in jail and dying in 1944 of his last imprisonment.

Their creed, if any, was internationalism. Their involvement with Abyssinia, Spain, China and Czechoslovakia gave notice of the direction foreign policy would take when they had charge, as they seemed instinctively to know they would. They admired America and the Soviet Union for throwing off the feudal yoke and making peerless progress thereafter. They loved jazz and the hour of the Moscow broadcast in English, when my father did his spinning "so that I can hear of the collective farming of the Soviets while I ply the *charkha* of Gandhi Baba!" Their canvas was so multifarious, I missed out on dogma. Not for them one Path, one Book, one ism, the foaming mouth, the trance.

> Communism [*my father wrote in answer to my question*] . . . aims at producing a classless society where there are no rich and high and mighty who have all the good things and on the other hand a vast mass of ill-clad, ill-fed, ill-housed humanity. (Look at the contrast between the rich mill owners of Cawnpore, Bombay and Ahmedabad and their miserable "mill hands.") But between theory and practice there is a world of difference. You know the Sermon on the Mount and what a Christian should be like. Now watch the Christian English, French and Germans. And watch the Nazis and Communists tearing up the body of sorely stricken Poland, bravely fighting against overwhelming odds [*letter to the author from Ranjit Pandit, September 19, 1939*].

Edgar Snow, John Gunther, Eve Curie and others brought us the outside world. Historian Edward Thompson became a friend whose schoolboy son, Palmer (E.P. Thomson), my uncle sometimes wrote to. British Quakers and American missionaries were among those who backed freedom for India. We didn't just sit spellbound listening.

My sister, 12, gravely asked Margaret Sanger: "Don't you think we're well spaced!" and Mrs. Sanger who had failed to enthuse Mahatma Gandhi with contraception for the masses, was charmed.

Asia, from which European conquest had isolated us—cutting off ancient sea routes, opening up routes to serve Europe's insatiable appetites—represented more to the family than kinship and culture. On a world stage where everything not Greek in origin was more or less barbarian, where salvation was Jerusalem and glory meant Rome, they projected a faith whose highlights of intellect, aspiration and embattled peasant courage were Asian.

They were confident inter-Asian problems would find wise mature solutions. Was this how "the subject races" coped with the ruthless destruction of their economies, the falsification of their histories, the imposition of Europe's gun-barrel view? Did their yearning invent an Asia to match Europe's myth of superiority?

Did the family invent the entire world? Theirs would not have fallen apart after the war, leaving its people at the mercy of two terrifyingly armed blocks, and now one. Its borders, far from becoming porous, froze. Even as west Europe moved toward unity, invisible barbed wire and broken glass proclaimed For Europeans Only, while tiny murderous nationalisms splintered the east. No just or generous order was established. The market to be served was still somewhere else. The ocean depths and sky were part of it. To go your way left you behind in a race you had no wish to join, whose ultimatum was: Join or die. Did we come all this way, I hear the family ask, to get baited, hooked and fried all over again?

They would have mourned the renaming of Leningrad, and been surprised by the demolition of a church whose message, along with Gandhi's, had made them as invincible as they were.

Now that it had repented of its tyrannies and seen the light, by what rationale did communism deserve to be trashed when, the evil deeds of other religions notwithstanding, religion was still in use?

The collapse of basic assumptions about their own republic would have appalled them. In their own, somehow prescient, "tryst with destiny," they never foresaw the bloody combine of religious, ethnic and secessionist savagery that would butcher, among thousands of others, two whose calculatedly shredded remains would hardly make respectable corpses for their state funerals.

But had they known they would have insisted the proposition that is "India" is our most civilized achievement in six thousand years, not to be destroyed by any variation of the foaming mouth, the trance. If they were told it's happening everywhere, countries are fracturing, there's only one ism now, and it's carnival time for fanatics, they would repeat:

But friends and comrades, this is India. Hold on.

Admittedly the view from the domed house, and its India, were strange for their sanity.

Addresses
at
Literary and Academic Conferences

India's Identity in *Mistaken Identity*

When I arrived two days ago in London, from Dehra Dun where I live in India, I was struck all over again by the almost planetary difference between these two worlds, and the fact that in spite of a surface likeness developing between different parts of the world, in spite of fax and telex and look-alike towns and the similarity of advertising and all the rest, there are vast, deep, unexplored sub-surfaces with agendas of their own, whole floating worlds beneath the surface of the ruling western agenda. These come to the surface every now and then. They burst through in opposition to the western agenda in such manifestations as, for example, religious fundamentalism, by which they try to hold their own, hold on to what they consider their identity. And aside from fanaticisms, there are whole positive agendas that are still waiting to come to light.

And it seems to me that these differences, visible and invisible, are growing rather than dissolving, so that a person like me who belongs in a sense to both worlds, finds it increasingly difficult to reconcile the two. On a personal level the western world I grew up in is no longer there. Its map, its ideology, its priorities have changed. At the same time the Indian world I grew up in is also no longer there, for the stage is set for every kind of religious and other combat and confrontation with the ideas that produced modern India. Quite frankly, I don't know where I'm going, which means I don't know what I will say in my next novel, or how I will resolve the growing chasm between my two worlds when I next put pen to paper. Because so far I've always gone along on the theory—and in the belief—that likenesses would grow. Now I don't know if they will, or if they can, and whether in future I will have to concoct an imaginary space to write about, since the spaces I knew aren't there any more.

I suppose this concerns me somewhat because my continuing character is India and my books have been about contemporary hopes and fears, set in political situations, and the implications of political

* Address at Women Writer's Workshop, Commonwealth Institute, London, on February 12, 1993

events on people's lives. But if India herself basically changes—and of course there have been many gradual, and some sudden, shifts over the years which I have recorded, then will I become a sort of emotional exile on my own soil? Asian writing nowadays covers a wide perspective and range of issues, and spreads across continents. But if you are, and always have been, rooted to one spot, of pure choice, and the ground beneath your feet starts sliding apart, then it makes for some interesting speculation as to what exactly you are going to be standing on thereafter.

Mistaken Identity, the novel I'm going to talk about, is as much about India's identity as the plight of its counter-hero, Bhushan Singh, who suddenly finds himself taken off a train in the middle of the night and carted off to jail, where he is imprisoned along with several Communists, and followers of Mahatma Gandhi, for no reason he can understand. India's identity is not related merely to a land mass, or defined in terms of her territory and boundaries. She has, to me, been a unique proposition based on the most civilized human instincts—a sort of meeting place of the human race, where the search for identity has worked itself out, by and large peacefully and creatively, through different traditions of music and dance, arts and crafts, food, speech, poetry, dress and manners, in fact all that goes into distinguishing one lifestyle from another. There is a recognition in this process that there is no end to the debt we owe strangers, and that what we call Motherland itself owes much to the contribution of strangers. This is a notion of a *collective selfhood*, not a mystical identity we were born into, but the fruit of our conscious labour and striving, built by our conscious endeavour. It not only means what we are, but what we hope to become, because a nation is the end result of *all* the influences that have been brought to bear upon its people, social and economic no less than spiritual. And of course all of this acquires a poignant meaning now that it is under attack, and now that an attempt is being made to deconstruct India into a purely Hindu identity, and squeeze her into this single mould. Two days after I get back to India the Hindu party threatens to hold a million-strong demonstration in Delhi to prove the strength of this demand, and if it succeeds in capturing power we will be well and truly in the snakepit of fundamentalism. But that is a nightmare that I hope will not come to pass, for I hope the political institutions we have built since independence, the social, psychological and emotional attitudes that are common to us all, and the reverence we share for the spirit of religion, will bring us through this crisis. Not least because the first victims of any kind of religious fundamentalism are women. It is when the times are judged ripe enough that feudal, reactionary and bigoted forces raise their heads to crush and control women and offer them up as various forms of human sacrifice. It is in the context of what modern India represents—a multicultural society that has long pulled off as of its very nature, what Yugoslavia has sadly been unable to, that I'm going to talk about *Mistaken Identity.*

1929, the year when the novel starts, is a year when revolutionary ideas inspired by men as unlike as Lenin and Mahatma Gandhi are spreading across India. There is industrial strife and political unrest. It is a particularly uncomfortable time for the British Raj which begins to unearth, or imagine, conspiracies against it and plots to overthrow the King Emperor. Arrests are made all over the country, men are thrown into jail or sent to the gallows, and a number of famous conspiracy trials take place. *Mistaken Identity* was inspired by one of these, in which a group imprisoned for about three years, is then released as no evidence is found against them. I feel particularly at home with a jail setting as my parents were so often in jails and the atmosphere comes naturally to me.

Alongside this upheaval is feudal India, the India of the landlords, where life goes on as before. Nationalism and communism are distant thunder to this leisured landed distocracy who live in a Never Land of their own. They devote their time and energy to lawsuits, to the patronage of poets and musicians, to great refinements of dress and manners, to acquiring new horses and elephants, carriages and cars, and raising their tenants' rents to pay for these, but above all, to the pursuit of titles and honours from the British Government, from jewelled robes and swords, and order of presentation at audiences with the Governor or the Viceroy, through the hierarchy of titles, topped by the coveted hereditary title of Raja. The landlords are the rent-receiving intermediaries between the British Government and the Indian peasantry, and their power over the peasantry is absolute. They are little emperors in their own domains and they live and behave like absolute monarchs. The landlord system existed, of course, under Moghul rule, too, but it had been based then more on corporate ties of clan, kith and kin. Under the British a new style of landlord was created who collected revenue for them and vied with other landlords for British favour. The British believed this competitive quest for status would keep them busy and make them less likely (after the Mutiny) to unite against the Government. So the landlord, like the moneylender, soon became the classic villain of Indian fiction and cinema, and in any case a sort of landmark in a countryside impervious to change.

Within this feudal setup the women were in purdah and their apartments, known as the *zenana*, were blocked off by high walls. Their business was to produce sons, and female infanticide, once widely practised, was still surreptitiously practised in the 20th century. This, along with child marriage and polygamy, was taken for granted.

The culture of the landed gentry was Moghul and they harked back nostalgically to the glory of that era. Urdu and Persian were spoken by Hindu and Muslim landlords alike. The business of the estate was conducted in Urdu. Though some devout Hindus stayed away from Islamic culture, it was generally a shared culture, even in the region I am writing about—Ayodhya—the heartland of Hinduism which Hindu fundamentalists have now converted into a battlefield.

In this background of revolutionary upheaval alongside the time-warp of feudal life, I've set the story of Bhushan Singh, handsome son of a wealthy landlord himself. Bhushan Singh is a loafer, a delinquent and a failed poet who resembbles Rudolph Valentino and has a way with women. He gets arrested and dumped into jail, by mistake of course, along with a group of nationalists and communists, and has to stand trial with them during the course of three years. He, and we, discover that his sentence may have something to do with his karma, and not with the crime of trying to overthrow the King Emperor, of which he is accused. He is something of a curiosity to his fellow prisoners, and as a way of passing time, and studying the oddity in their midst, they ask him to tell them about his home and upbringing. So Bhushan Singh becomes a Scheherezade, describing, and in the process re-living, his past.

He is a man obsessed, obsessed with a lost love. The Muslim girl he had a youthful affair with, was then disappeared by her family, presumably into a cruel arranged marriage. His affair with her triggered a Hindu-Muslim riot and Bhushan Singh's banishment to college in America, but his love for her remains an obsession with him, and the novel is about his search for Razia. From America—where he has whiled away his time learning the Turkey Trot and other dances of the 1920s and making love to Willie Mae Goldburger, the sex-starved daughter of a movie magnate—he returns to live in Bombay, as his father does not want him on the estate, and there he has a long and loving relationship with a Parsi beauty called Sylla before he finally comes to the end of his search and finds himself inexplicably in jail.

What is the story 'about'? Well, it's about obsession, or as Bhushan Singh's mother calls it, 'love-madness,' which distinguishes an obsessive love from the ordinary variety. It is about demented, besotted love, the kind mystics have for God, and sometimes men and women have for each other. It is about the fact that we find what we are looking for, though not always in the way we expect, or that suits us. It's also about an India struggling for freedom, and the kind of lifelong commitment all kinds of people gave to this fight. And it is about a belief in an India where there is no Hindu and no Muslim, only a shared tradition created and enriched by a fabulous joint culture, by people who have lived as good neighbours side by side for centuries. This broad universal approach is in fact the meaning of being Indian, for India is a many-faceted diamond reflecting all the light and splendour that has come her way.

Then it is also about the fact that there is no pure race and no such thing as ethnic purity; that cultures have crisscrossed and bloodstreams have mingled so that this interweave can never again be unwoven. The human race is mixed. It is impure. The individual Indian's life experience is certainly composed of different cultural strands, and has to be, on a subcontinent that has been repeatedly invaded and occupied. He is a product of numerous visible and invisible influences. Identity on Indian soil, far from being traceable to a single source, as all fundamentalists insist, has acquired endless ramifications, as I suspect it has on every other soil. So all talk of purity and superiority is nonsense everywhere. There can be no deliberate deconstruction of any country, certainly not India, into one exclusive identity. The idea is as much a hallucination as Hitler's theory of a pure race was, or ideas of ethnic cleansing today, or indeed ideas of keeping Europe a white fortress. I think of this novel as a hymn to racial impurity, and in praise of the mixtures that have combined to produce the modern Indian, in this case with the interlocking of two traditions, Hindu and Muslim, within an individual life.

What this book is most significantly about is two women in purdah, Bhushan Singh's Hindu mother, and his Muslim beloved, Razia, who against all the extraordinary odds achieve triumphant liberation, flowering and fulfillment. There is no hero in this story but there are two heroines, the kind of remarkable women a society like India produces, whose inner strength and determination to be free are more than a match, ultimately, for all the chains that bind them and the forces that act as fetters on them.

And finally I should say that though Bhushan Singh is no hero, he is a man with a lover's instinct, not merely for women but for the hybrid culture that has bred him. As such he is probably the need of the hour, any hour. He is a failure. He is hopelessly unambitious, with no desire to achieve anything other than union once again with his beloved, but after all, we've seen what the earth's great achievers and their flaming ambitions can make of it. Maybe the loafers do less harm, especially those with a vision of communal harmony and human unity. I confess I have a great and growing sympathy with men like Bhushan Singh. He's man who recognizes the fact that his real talent is for ballroom dancing.

He recognizes and revels in the strength and ardour of his women. Hinduism and Islam meet in him, in ways both practical and mysterious. He personifies the legend of Kabir, the 15th century weaver-poet. When Kabir died, his Hindu and Muslim followers, quarrelling over whether to cremate or bury his corpse, lifted the shroud to find only flowers in place of his body, his own sublime answer that he belonged to both communities and no power or prejudice could imprison him within one confining label. The legend lives on in Bhushan Singh for whom there are not merely these two communities that we as Indians partake of, but that we are indeed each other, joined from the gut, and that this, in essence, is the full-blooded meaning of India.

Illusion and Reality*

I can only share with you some thoughts I have on the collection of islands and continents we call the world, which are the subject of this conference, and to talk about some ideas that have governed this world and their effects on us, for it is my belief that writing comes as much out of this heritage as the heritage known as a literary tradition.

I have to speak personally, and as an Indian. How else can one speak, except from one's own time, experience and position, with all the limitations that these impose? And when I say 'we' or 'us,' I am referring to the people who lie more or less within the same general ambit of experience, and share a somewhat similar outlook in common. And in these very broad general terms it seems to me that the 'we' I speak of are the people who live out scenarios that have been conceived elsewhere, and been directed from that elsewhere by other people. The real world we have been repeatedly told we live in has not been one whose reality we could believe in. For us, it has been a stage set by others on which we have played the roles assigned to us.

The imperial era I was born into was a stage setting of this kind. Empire itself was no illusion. It was a fact of life, a businesslike arrangement that had divided up the globe into rulers and the ruled, masters and slaves. Under this dispensation huge land masses with names and ancient civilizations of their own became quaintly known as Europe's 'possessions,' and hung with European ownership titles: British India, Dutch East Indies, French Indo China, German East Africa and so on. Trade routes opened up by these owners carried everything from silk and spices to human flesh westward. All this went on for several hundred years and it was real enough. But the proposition that this scenario was based on was probably the most ingenious and imaginative fiction we have ever heard, mythologizing Europe as the centre of the world, inhabiting it with a superior race, and bestowing upon it a monopoly of civilization, all of which then gave it the right to conquer

---

* Keynote Address at ACLALS Conference "Islands and Continents" at Colombo on 14 August 1995

and make use of non-Europe for its profit and pleasure. Non-Europe in this scenario was a mixed bag of 'lesser breeds'—a wonderfully expressive phrase immortalized by the imperial poet, Kipling, and these 'lesser breeds' were long overdue for European enlightenment.

These flights of fantasy would have faded like the fantasies they were, if they had not yielded so much profit, and had not therefore been glued and hammered into place with blood and iron, and legitimized by a massive scaffolding of words and images and pseudo-scientific theories in their support. Generations grew up and died doomed to inferiority, believing there was no way out of this scenario which posed as a true and natural state of affairs. And outdated and hackneyed though this situation now sounds, it is so very recent that South Africa struggled out of its stranglehold only a few years ago.

What difference can this or any other outer casing make to our lives? Does the lie that others impose on us as history affect ordinary people's on-going lives? Does it affect the aromas of your grandmother's cooking, or the sound of rain on your roof, or your love for your beloved? And aren't these basically what the human process is all about? Yet it is this outer casing that becomes the framework we are compelled to act within, and travel through, burdened with itineraries that may or may not be of our own choosing, but that nevertheless dominate our journey, and colour our mentality. And history does dog our footsteps, even and especially those of us who have left our soil of origin and acquired new nationalities. When has the kind of world we lived in not moved into us, even though we might not even be aware of its major events and upheavals? The mentality that flourished in a flat world was quite different from the grander one that dawned on a globe whose seas men could navigate, and still grander is it now that we live in a boundless cosmos holding worlds upon worlds still waiting to be discovered. Our outer casing affects us powerfully, and we are squaring our account with it in big and intimate ways every day of our lives. In fact, in our own era the line between public and private has been a continually disappearing one, as vast numbers of people have had to face the traumatic consequences of public events in their private lives. The gap between public and private is in any case infinitesimal in all societies that are in transition. When politics enters daily life, those who write, among others, are forced to take sides, and it becomes impossible to separate politics from literature or any other department of life. In such an environment literature would be floating in a void if it did not enter the arena.

When great areas of the world were released from the cast-iron outer casing of empire, the horizon was revealed, the skies expanded, and we came out of our silences. The first thing this set us free to do was to speak, from points of view based on assumptions and findings that had had no hearing till then. We had something of value to contribute: a point of view—another way of looking at the world, an alternative art of politics, of love and marriage, of medicine, philosophy and nutrition. We believed these alternative approaches might even lead to some useful shifts in perspective, and would find their due place in the mainstream of affairs which until then had been undilutedly western. But at this moment another scenario invented elsewhere was launched on us. The bombs dropped on Hiroshima and Nagasaki had let loose a reign of terror in the shape of an escalating arms race that kept the world on the brink of a third world war as the two Super Powers matched weapon for weapon, and fought out their rivalries in proxy wars all over the map. One of them made a hell on earth for ten years in Vietnam, and one of their proxy wars has reduced Afghanistan to ruin and destitution. The illusion on which all this devastation and destruction was founded was that two ideologies could not co-exist. It had to be either-or.

For those of us who did not see life in these black and white categories, or see peace in terms of an armed race and armed camps, it was all rather bewildering. The armed camp called the Free World which the non-aligned were being persuaded to join looked like a cocktail of dictatorships and theocracies besides democracies. But apart from this, taking sides made no sense to those who did not *want* to restrict themselves to the *either* or the *or* on offer. We felt kindly toward both, and though each camp warned us of the evils of the other, we hobnobbed with both the capitalists and the communists and felt both were necessary for a world in need of more than one solution. In India we had a hoary tradition of communal living and common ownership of land and individual enterprise. We had no intention of becoming a trophy of either camp by joining its military alliances. But like it or not, and even if one rejected the straitjacket of either-or, everyone had to revolve around the remarkable fiction that the human race is too tiny to accommodate two ideas.

Khruschev once told a joke against himself at a dinner party at the Indian embassy in Moscow. He said he had been touring the country and had come across an ancient ragged peasant. He thumped him on the back and asked him, "Well, grandfather, and how has life been treating you since the Great October Revolution?" The ancient one said miserably, "*Look* at me, comrade. Before the Great October Revolution I had two coats to wear. Since the revolution I've had only this one, and it is so tattered it is falling off my back." Khruschev said heartily,

"Count your blessings, grandfather. Do you know there are countries in the world where people are running around naked because they have absolutely nothing to wear?" The peasant gave a gloomy nod and said, "In that case, comrade, they must have had *their* Great October Revolution long before ours."

I wasn't there on the occasion but I have wondered why on earth Khruschev didn't come to the adult conclusion that it was time to compromise, and give the Great October Revolution a hefty dose of rugged individualism. He might have saved his country from collapse, as America would have saved itself decades of paranoia if it had admitted there was another view of world affairs besides its own.

A scene from Satyajit Ray's film *Pratidwandi* illustrates the point of view many of us were in sympathy with at the time. In the film the hero appears for a job interview. The interviewer asks him what, in his opinion, is man's greatest modern achievement. He replies that it is the heroism of the Vietnamese. As this is the time when Neil Armstrong has just landed on the moon, one of the interviewers asks him why he has placed Vietnamese valour above the moon landing, and he says the moon landing is a triumph of technology, while Vietnam is a triumph of the human spirit.

The either-or hysteria came to an end when the Soviets opened up their system. With glasnost and perestroika it collapsed of its own weaknesses, and the Soviet Union disintegrated under its new pressures. But no sooner had this happened when we were ushered into yet another version of reality that many of us are having a hard time subscribing to, which is that unrestrained competition holds the key to the kingdom of heaven, and the Lord has proven this by vanquishing communism. This latest figment of imagination from elsewhere is being fitted into place by a process known as the globalization of markets, and the market mantra is now the law. It is now the outer casing, the current interpretation of history that we are having to live within.

There is nothing wrong with globalization. Who doesn't want to be part of a changing world, and reap the benefits thereof? But which world? Is it going to be one we can still recognize ourselves in, and have had some little share in designing? As things stand, we are not even sure of a welcome in some parts of it. In spite of all we hear about boundaries dissolving, never did boundaries look solider than they do now, with immigration barriers rising higher and racism taking to the streets. The perils of passage through those barriers, and once through them, the perils of arrival, are not so far items that the globalizers have included on their agenda. Maybe that is yet to come, but so far the agenda is not startlingly new. In a manner of speaking, colonization was a form of globalization. It built roads and railways, opened sea routes and extended communications to connect up the empire and speed up commerce. Today it is not a one-way process. The globalizers of markets have to consult national sovereignties and seek permissions. Some of their former possessions have become economies to reckon with. There is discussion and bargaining in international forums. But it revolves around the ground rules laid down by the financial institutions of the west, and it is they who carry the day. And industrial interests are so heavily backed by their governments that aid can be withdrawn and sanctions imposed when markets cannot be had for the asking, and when access to a vital commodity such as oil looks threatened, governments think nothing of going to war, as they did in the Gulf.

Within this compulsory marketization of the world, which a friend of mine calls market terrorism, our colonized minds are still hung over with older inflictions. Concepts like modernization and development have automatically been taken to mean what the west understands by them. Levels of industry and technology are judged by western standards. Non-Europe, without its own criteria, has no option but to struggle on in imitation of the models and standards set up in the west. This has its own fallout in poor societies. But apparently this is a race that now has to be run, and in circumstances where essential power, from finance to information and armaments, is largely controlled by the west. The nuclear club, with its one non-western member, is a particularly terrifying monopoly. How it can demand a ban on the proliferation of nuclear weapons when it refuses to disarm itself, is hard to understand, since the only way to prevent the spread of weapons is by universal disarmament. And why nuclear arsenals should be considered safe in the hands of these club members—one of whom is the only country to have put these bombs to actual use—is another bit of reasoning that is hard to fathom. Old sins have long shadows, and the shadows of the bombs dropped on Hiroshima and Nagasaki still lie over us, with the race for nuclear arms continuing, and armaments a thriving industry without whose sales the prosperous economies would be much less prosperous. The world is not a cosy place at this point in time. Who can rest easy in such a world?

And who can rest assured that the redrawing of maps has made it a world where all human beings have equal status? A few months ago, on the 50th anniversary of the end of World War II, I watched programmes about the holocaust. There was also an official apology from Germany for this crime. I was curious about what slant and coverage would be given to the anniversary of Hiroshima. It was mentioned in the news, of course, but the horrific aspect of the atomic bombs was ignored.

Though Japan had expressed remorse for its aggression and its wartime oppression of Asian nations, no international leader was present at the ceremony at the memorial, and only a junior United Nations official. And far from there being an apology from the United States for the worst genocide of all time, there were justifications of the event, and a celebration of a golden anniversary, the 50th birthday of the atom bomb. Apparently no one need apologize for exterminating the 'lesser breeds.' You will forgive me if I can't think of this world as globalized. And if you ask me what all this has to do with an ACLALS conference, and the field of literature, I would have to say, what else is consciousness composed of but the age it lives in, and if writers do not in some way reflect that age, what are they writing about?

The aim of globalization seems to be the creation of a mono-culture, so that every place on earth will end up looking like Kansas City. The metaphor of Kansas City occurred to me because of the song in the musical, *Oklahoma*, which goes: "Everything's up-to-date in Kansas City, they've gone about as far as they can go." But this is that brand of packaged programmed change that makes short work of history and continuity, and if you have a lot of those, you have a lot to lose. Once the varieties of human culture have been transformed into varieties of tourism, what need is there for memory? That is the process we, in my part of the world, seem to be caught in, and never did an outer casing make such zombies of us, take hold of body, brain and entrails as fast as this one shows every sign of doing. Globalization of this sort looks like one more form of fundamentalism because it sees itself as the one and only way ahead, the only path to progress, when we know very well that nothing of the sort can be true. The oldest wisdom is that there is no single wisdom. Take the matter of diet. The experts keep coming to us with different rules but no one has yet said the last word on what's good for us. Every other day the last word changes. There's a story about a diet researcher who went to interview a 90-year-old man and asked him how he accounted for his longevity. The 90-year-old raised a trembling finger and said, "No drop of liquor ever touched my lips." The researcher wrote this down and then asked how the old gentleman could put up with all the noise coming from upstairs, the singing and dancing and yelling, and the 90-year-old shrugged, "Oh, that's just Dad, drunk as usual."

It seems to me that I've always lived in a world according to elsewhere. The concepts it was based on, the point of view it held, were taught to me in textbooks, not as the west's contribution to knowledge, but as indisputable knowledge, and canonized as truths. These were not only the political scenarios written elsewhere. There have been all kinds of scenarios, resting on all kinds of assumptions, that had no particular validity for us, but which all too often we did not challenge or question, not just because they came from that fashionable, powerful and influential elsewhere, but because there seemed no exit from it, no other intellectual space to move in. Let's take the example of psychology, since Freud and Jung and psychoanalysis have dominated life and literature in this century. Why should we be blown before them like leaves in a wind? *Are* Greek myths, and Oedipus and other complexes, really pivotal to our understanding of our sexual natures? Are there perhaps other ways of exploring states of consciousness? Why not let those in elsewhere sort out their problems with their sons and lovers on psychiatrists' couches, or spill their guts out on television talk shows? What reason is there to be trapped in an alien point of view? And if this is an age known as post-modern, then wouldn't post-modern, like modern, perhaps have a different meaning and implications for us than these concepts have in elsewhere, where they originated? Concepts travel, and travel changes them. Feminism is a case in point. Though autonomy is the goal of women's struggles for equality everywhere, issues of sheer survival and basic human needs give ours a more tormenting dimension.

Again, what is so final or inevitable or attractive, for *us*, about the economic system that western post-modernism has laid down, complete with its structure, its goals and its values? Do we really go along with an ideology of no-holds-barred competition, and aggressive individualism, in which family, community, the contacts and responsibilities between generations, the welfare of the weak and vulnerable, play no part? Is it really possible that man is an endless consumer whose happiness lies in endless consumption; that more and more toys must be produced for him to play with; that in effect he's no better than a grunting pig with gargantuan appetites, and stuffing those appetites is the right and proper way for him live? These theories are not alien only to non-Europe. The idea that life is nourished on greed and grab and there is no moral law beyond material satisfactions, must be repugnant to every society on earth. How and why such notions have found gurus and disciples I cannot say—though these *are* times when all manner of bizarre cults find huge followings—but obviously this particular cult has to be knocked out of existence, laughed out of court, so that if history has indeed come to a stop, as an American academic would have us believe, we can get it going again without delay, and human beings can resume their march to a more civilized level of living, and out of the pigs' trough they have been shoved into by the new economic philosophers.

Quite apart from history being allowed to go on, it would be nice if literature went on too. Will it? I wonder if, those who write will be able to disassociate themselves from any outer wrappings they find uncomfortable, so that they can feel free to transmit their own individual perceptions. Empires, after all, were unmade not merely by new arrangements of words on a page, but the new visions and intensities felt through them. Black immigrant literatures have hacked life and laughter and lyricism out of the unrelenting societies around them by exercising their own independent imaginations and not the ghosts of others. But these achievements took for granted the preservation of an inner freedom in the absence of external freedom. Great works have come out of unfree conditions, as in 19th century Russia, the Soviet Union, East Europe or Latin America. Whether it can happen in India, in the future that is now upon us, I don't know. I don't live in a metropolitan centre and I try *not* to keep up with trends, but the impression I have is that the Indian elite are entranced with the excitement of eating a potato chip made with French collaboration, and buying a Maidenform bra. I should explain that until recently India had severely restricted imports in order to build up her own industrial infrastructure, so the flood of foreign goods is a novelty. To judge by the glittering goods advertised, and their skyrocketing prices, or by the magazine articles and TV programmes about the rich and famous, whose celebrity rests on how many times a year they pop over to Paris or New York, one could easily come to the conclusion that we are a jet-propelled society, living in a limbo of limitless luxury, and that there's no such place as India any more.

Instead of the crackle of ideas there once was, inanity rules the day. Newspapers are remaking themselves to become more marketable, and since markets don't need editors, this disappearing breed has gone into other media jobs and been replaced by marketing managers. Publishers, like some of their counterparts elsewhere, have become purveyors of merchandise. And the electronic media, which now has a unique opportunity to use the latest technology to project the themes and images that concern us, is giving impeccable imitations of tasteless fare from the west. The pornography hitting the market follows suit, and this is truly disappointing as one had expected something more original than the regulation nude centrefolds, and what the textile tycoon's ex-mistress told her rival after their fourth double scotch on the rocks. From the inheritors of Kama Sutra, Khajuraho, and other sophisticated splendours in word and stone, one had hoped for a touch of class. But just as Macdonald's rubbery hamburger may soon drive the sublime shami kebab out of the market, our pornographers have settled for dreary derivative porn instead of blazing a new trail. As we were once interpreted by others through the lenses of the Raj, we are now interpreting ourselves in the jargon, and by the norms and market values, of globalization. As a child I was once shown the newspaper picture of Mahatma Gandhi striding up the stairs of Buckingham Palace in his loincloth, for a meeting with His Majesty the King. Looking back, there is a magnificence about that picture. It seems to symbolize how two cultures *should* meet, each with its dignity and integrity intact.

The Indian scene is much more Indian than the zombie-like rush for buying, selling and mimicking, hallowed by the media and the advertisers, would have us believe. Our virtues and our vices are all our own. Politics, once an altar for self-sacrifice and idealism, now offers dazzling criminal opportunities. The classic villains of fiction and cinema in the 1930s and 40s—the landlords, the moneylenders, the priests—begin to look like babes in arms compared with the dashing new breed. Then we've got militant Hinduism, two words which since time began could never be linked because they were mutually contradictory. Now efforts are being made to join them by politicians who are busy rewriting Indian history, and to listen to the chitchat on the lawns and in the bars of exclusive clubs, about eight hundred years of Hindu-Muslim culture might never have existed. There have been changes at every level, the major one being convulsions in the caste structure that have stood the caste system on its head. The once backward castes govern states, and control positions of wealth and power. The western-educated high caste elite to whom the British transferred power in 1947 have long since had their day. The several hundred million Indians blotted out by the advertisers are demonstrating their clout in ways we like and don't like. Will the writers among us have a sense of the history that has brought all this about? Will they say anything of all this? Will we carry the awareness that will translate into what we alone have to offer, and not just into cleverness and special effects?

The best writers in the west have their national and group experiences branded into them—their French and Russian and American revolutions, their golden ages and disasters. We were branded, by training in their histories and literatures and methodologies, more with their experiences than our own. But this was a condition that was passing, when the current known as globalization swept us on the road to Kansas City, and swept everything from sausages to writing into the same market-value production line. Gobbled into this new framework from elsewhere, what can a pen put on paper but words that have no past, and probably very little future? There may well be words that will attract investment in the industry that writing has become; words that may take us backward, concocting versions of the orient as it is still expected to be, complete with ethnic flourishes and misty mysticisms and bags of tricks. The Indian writer, Mulk Raj Anand, points out the contrast in angle of vision between his own story of an orphan in his novel *Coolie*, who is a real Indian orphan, and Kipling's colourful fantasy character, Kim, who helps the British to protect their Indian empire from the Russians. Will we be back to variations of *Kim*? Or, will we be seduced by the mechanized, globalized words and images spawned by the new technologies, and divorced from our own context and conditions? For people whose main resource is their imagination, technology may reserve its most death-dealing devices. I know technology is sacrosanct, and has been written into the scripture of what is known as progress, but there must be a point beyond which we do not let it usurp our human functions, and that point may well have been reached. But mesmerized by it, will we in India well and truly return to being creatures of elsewhere?

I am reminded of a friend of mine years ago in Bombay, a cultivated, elegant, much admired woman. There was something about her that used to puzzle me, that I couldn't quite place, until I realized that if I closed my eyes and shut out her dark skin and her sari, and thought of her as an upper class Englishwoman, everything about her fell into place. In India the old order died no violent death. It was bowed out. In the drawing rooms of Bombay high society in the late 1950s, it was still very much around. My friend charmingly reflected its accent, its conversation, its culture. These were the masks Indians had once worn in order to be invited to the ball as it were, to be acceptable in ruling circles, and a good many of them had never taken them off. Maybe they had become a second skin and they felt more comfortable with them than with the Indian reality around them, or maybe their indoctrination had made them incapable of a relationship with India, except as outsiders, and unfit for any role except one in a masquerade. I told her once that I had been to the airport to receive Ho Chi Minh and found him one of the gentlest and most affectionate of men, and this filled her with genuine amazement, for she genuinely believed he was a monster. She also believed India was not going to last out the next decade. The country was going to fall apart. A foreign think-tank had told her so. Thus, when we wear masks, do the demons of others become our demons, and their gods, our gods. And I have an overwhelming sense of deja vu today as I look around me when I go to Delhi, which is more advanced in matters of globalization than Dehra Dun, where I live. It seems to me we are yet again acting and reacting within the confines of a provided framework. Perhaps it is still a case of having to wear a mask or not being invited to the ball. It is certainly still the case that the journeys we make continue to take us westward, to what is still the centre of the world.

It is these journeys to what is still the centre of the world, a Mecca even in our own consciousness, that create the illusion that because varieties of people flock to that Mecca, we are now living in a cosmopolitan era; that literature, too, is becoming cosmopolitan, unfettered by frontiers or a frontier consciousness, and that it no longer needs to start from a place of its own. This bit of logic is like the Miss Universe contest, which chooses the most beautiful woman in the universe from twenty-one glamorous contestants, after which she goes on to advertise Coca Cola. The word cosmopolitan similarly covers a handful compared with the mass of people who feel at home only in a particular soil, many of them untouched by outer trends. 'Cosmopolitan' has about it the exclusive luxurious tinkle of privileged culture. When I hear that the world is fast becoming cosmopolitan, or that it is now a global village, I feel I must be living in another world, not the one all the experts are talking about. And I think this is entirely possible since it is far from being One World.

Speaking at an ACLALS conference a few years ago I asked when post-colonial would stop being post-colonial. Now I wonder when exile stops being exile. I'm not sure I understand the word the way it is now used, to cover so many variations on the theme. I have come across book reviews referring to the book's author as exiled. Recently I came across a book which was partly about the effects of exile on writers and their writing. The dictionary definition, which is banishment, or long absence from one's country, would not fit them all. Can exile, when it is the result of choosing to live somewhere else, be exile? Can such a person's state of mind and being, however nostalgic, in any way resemble the sense of displacement and loss that plagues those who have been forced to leave home, as political or economic refugees? Can the label of exile be pinned on all expatriate writing? I read very little, and I know nothing about the vocabulary of criticism, so I may be quite wrong in thinking that the word exile has acquired a cult flavour, and come to have extravagant all purpose meanings, almost as if Rupert Murdoch, on acquiring American nationality, had become an exile.

In 1992, the *Guardian* published a series of articles under the heading "Writing Home," in which writers around the world reflected on their nationality, and described their feelings for the country they called home. I thought I would find in these articles a rejection of the sentiment people once attached to their native soil, even a thankfulness at having shed all that, either metaphorically, or by literally moving to new territory. I thought my own contribution to the series would show up an unfashionable attachment to my roots in an age when cross-cultural connections are supposed to matter more than roots. I thought I would be in a minority of one. To my surprise there were several like me, for whom a national identity was not only *not* out-of date, but a source of selfhood. Two of these writers, with opportunities to settle in the west, decided to remain in their authoritarian homelands. The Chinese writer, Zhang Xianliang, had spent 22 years in a labour camp and was still not being published in China, yet these are his words:

> Perhaps there are some who belong to the world and not to one country. I cannot be such a person. In my body and spirit I can belong only to China. I do not believe that there can be a truly universal literature which is not attached to any particular society. Even Shakespeare's works belong in the end to England.

The Czech writer, Ivan Klima, was visiting London when Soviet troops invaded Czechoslovakia, but he went home. In his words:

> home, where at any moment the police could ring the doorbell and search my flat, take me off for interrogation or even arrest me. Home where my wife was continually getting the sack, where I didn't know whether my children would be allowed to study, and where I was banned from publishing. . . . But I was born here and have accepted it as destiny that my home is here. The worst thing for me would be to discover that my home is nowhere, or that it is everywhere, which is no more than a substitute for . . . 'nowhere,' and is intended to fill more easily that empty space in the soul which the loss of home tends to leave behind.

Likewise, Shusako Endo of Japan, who writes about the suffering of the Japanese during the war, the horror of the atomic strikes, the humiliation of defeat, and what Japan has lost in the race to become an industrialized power, concludes: "However, as a Japanese, I cannot desert Japan." And Chinua Achebe of Nigeria, who had no choice but to leave Nigeria if he wanted to stay alive, writes: "The hard words Nigeria and I have said to each other look like words of anxious love, not hate." Shusako Endo also writes: "Many Japanese—especially the young—are gripped by a sense of emptiness. One manifestation of this is the . . . large number of people travelling overseas." It would seem that the plant of universalism, at least according to these writers, is itself a product of having stayed rooted. And incidentally, I've often wondered what sort of books Henry James would have written if *he'd* stayed home during the wonderful turbulent years of America's tremendous growth as a nation.

True cosmopolitanism, which would mean partaking of a world culture, cannot exist, there being no world culture, only the Europe-centeredness that substitutes for one. On the other hand, wars of identity rage all about us, including here on this once serene island, and few are as fortunate as Naipaul in being able to sort out their enigmas of identity in peaceful, affluent surroundings. Those countries of Europe that are the most advanced and stable areas of the world are just as fiercely obsessed with their identity, and with keeping their racial identity unsullied, when they pass laws to restrain or prohibit non-white immigration. Whether identity bares its teeth and claws in actual battle, or dresses soberly and speaks in suave accents, or is simply the need within us to stay home, it is very much with us.

But if all I have said sounds like a plea for nationalism, my plea is for the very opposite. Separateness is probably the most absurd and dangerous of all illusions. There never was a time when it was a sound idea. My own belief is in a reconciliation of cultures, of the sort that Nelson Mandela and Aung San Su Kyi have come to represent in politics. It is not time for me to become more like you, and to pattern myself on your ways, or to write what pleases you. What it is time for is for us to harmonize our ways of living and thinking, so that we will never be strangers to one another again; so that from a relationship that partakes of all our identities, a truly cosmopolitan world, and a genuinely universal literature, can arise.

An Aspect of Terror*

In a novel I wrote in 1972, called *The Day in Shadow*, a young divorced woman who is in difficulties over her crippling divorce settlement, and her life ahead, is having tea with an elderly friend, Ram Krishan, and this bit of dialogue takes place.

> 'Yes,' she said, 'I have wondered about that often. I have wished non-violence had become a way of thinking, made into a law, or given some kind of sanction, so that it could be passed on like an inheritance. I've wanted to pass it on to my son. Until one can, it's no use. . . . So that's why I have nothing to give my children, because I have nothing to give them except non-violence.'"
>
> Her laugh had a tremble to it. She went on talking nervously.
>
> 'I mean, how do you give them non-violence in an attractive package, something they can be sure will work in the world around them, unless they see it working first?'
>
> My dear, Ram Krishan wanted to say, my dear, don't be despairing. There is a world like that very near us, around the corner if you look for the signs. You in your lifetime may reach out and touch it, if you have the courage and the endurance, if you believe.

How absurdly irrelevant those words sound in an age that is probably more viciously violent, worldwide, than any age past. Twelve years after I wrote them, my cousin, who was then Prime Minister, was gunned to death by religious fanatics. Seven years later her son was shredded to pulp in a bomb blast by an ethnic fundamentalist. Yet in such times especially, what other remedy is there but non-violence? It is in any case the path of evolution, and the way tne world will be in time to come. But meanwhile there are ordeals by fire to be gone through,

---

* Plenary Address at Conference on "Terror: Its Representations and Politics," 9 April 1995, University of Kent, Canterbury.

some of long standing, and I want to talk about one of them which goes relentlessly on.

Most people do not belong to the European fold, to what still operates as the world's mainstream culture, but they live perforce in a world which is still dominated, in all vital particulars, by the west. This makes for a perverse situation, assigning the larger part of humanity to the position of a beleaguered minority. Psychologically this imposes a perpetual sense of isolation and otherness, and in practical affairs it continues to ignore or marginalize the many, leaving them little or no say in how the world is run, however damaging the course it takes may be to their lives, their health and their interests. Those outside the privileged and well-guarded frontiers of the mainstream not only have to put up with the routine humiliations thrust on them by racial arrogance, but with the aggressive forms that arrogance takes in trade, defence, immigration and other policies, and even in methods of warfare and peacemaking. The dividing line between Europe i.e. the west, and non-Europe seems designed to separate the human from subhuman species. It is specifically this, and not only the aggression and injustices involved, that I am calling an aspect of terror.

When a state of affairs has been as long established as western supremacy has been, it comes to be considered normal. The ancient world had slaves and free men. Jefferson's America declared all men equal, and no paradox was perceived in the fact that he, and perhaps other signatories to the declaration, owned hundreds of slaves. And almost up to the present time the world was divided into the ruling and the subject races. The long shadow of Europe, as concept and culture, loomed large, as of right, over human affairs, and the felt reality of being human, and of what constituted a human being, was a privilege claimed by that race and culture alone. Western dominance was not just the reigning political reality which one challenged, if at all, at one's own peril. It was enshrined as the normal, rational, and only possible state of affairs. Even those who opposed it found it hard to visualize any other kind of world order. Domestic relations came under somewhat the same dispensation when the physical and financial ownership of the wife by the husband was taken for granted. There are no circumstances so hard to dislodge, in public or private life, as those that look like a normal respectable condition.

Things have, of course, changed. No absolute dividing line now separates the rulers from the ruled. Some of the so-called subject races have crossed poverty lines and moved closer to western standards and life-styles. Some have become factors to reckon with, and the one-time rulers now include them. The rulers, too, cannot be lumped together.

They do not behave alike, nor do they represent a single monolithic point of view. There is probably no parallel to the voluntary withdrawal of the British from India, and few relationships between ruler and ruled have done as well as this one, including the efforts Britain is making to integrate her now multi-racial population. But by and large, equality and control over one's fate remain out of the reach of most, in a global arrangement where the west continues to occupy a vast political space by virtue of the fact that it controls the institutions of power: trade and industry, finance, information and armaments, and the technology that serves all these; and uses these levers as it sees fit, including war as a tool of policy, when a crucial commodity is involved, as in the Gulf War.

All this has been true in time past. Blood and commerce have gone together. It is what the violent history of imperialism was all about. But empires did not pretend otherwise, and they did not have the huge apparatus of modern technology at their disposal. Nor was economic adventure in the past able to bank on a philosophy of unbridled and undiluted consumerism as its rationale, or on greed as a desirable way of life. Now there are no ideological or moral restraints on the process. Wiped clean of debate or doubt, unimpeded by the more civilized aspects of a twentieth century conscience, commercial interests that are thousands of miles distant from the markets they target on the map, not only decide on the pressures to be used—sanctions, withdrawal of aid and loans, military strikes—but they do so by judging other societies, and the value of a human life in them, much as they did in the days of slavery and empire, by where they happen to be located on the map. And if this judgment then translates into international trade policies that are indifferent to the survival, livelihood, stability or self-respect of millions of people, so be it, since people who are not recognized as fellow human beings cannot be sinned against.

The jungle that goes by the name of commerce in any case knows no sin, but even the laws of the jungle have not been observed in double standards of industrial safety which have suddenly come to light when death-dealing disasters have taken place, like the gas explosion at the Union Carbide plant in Bhopal, India, which classically demonstrates the expendability of the poor. The compensation for a life lost has been about $1860, and to the injured about $540. Ten years after the event, those who are working for the welfare of its victims report an increase in respiratory disorders, cataracts, spontaneous abortions, TB and cancer cases.

It is also well known that pharmaceutical firms sell drugs in the Third World that are banned as dangerous by their own governments. And selective anti-environment and anti-human policies have been directly responsible for dislocation and impoverishment on a mass scale. On global warming, for which we are told the rich countries that overconsume the earth's natural resources are overwhelmingly responsible, one of the new economic philosophers has advised that nothing much need be done about it since the high-income countries can profitably adapt to it and in a hundred years its impact, on them will be negligible. In his words, "The winners will be happy, the losers will be miserable." According to a scientific forecast, these losers are expected to die in their tens of millions by the mid-21st century, but the economic advice to wait-and-see suits the multinational oil and coal industries, and we live in times when science plays second fiddle to profits. What will amount to a ferocious form of ethnic cleansing is permissible if it profits industry, and if those who are killed qualify racially as sacrificial victims. A similar "economic logic" justifies the dumping of toxic waste on African countries, which logic the former Chief Economist of the World Bank has called "impeccable." The powerless can expect no mercy, but if you happen to be a successful Asian competitor in any area of the market, you will find yourself up against measures unrelated to trade, to prevent your becoming a threat to industries in the west that cannot face competition.

The double standard governing intellectual property rights has an unmatched irony of its own. China's pirating of American software and other items has been much in the news. Reverse piracy and plunder are never heard about on the information networks that rule the skies. It's an idea I put into my novel *Mistaken Identity*: Comrade Dey is in jail in 1929 on the charge of a conspiracy to overthrow the King Emperor. He remarks to one of his fellow-prisoners, "Capitalists have a weird sense of proportion. Hours can be spent in their courts of law attacking and defending a man who has purloined a pen knife. But sail out and loot a country, bash up the population and make a scavengers' feast of their remains, and you go down in history as Something the Great."

But such is the chronic imbalance, and ingrained terrorism of a mentality that holds whole populations in contempt, and treats their countries as raw material to be recklessly exploited, at no matter what cost to human beings, and by financial intimidation or military intervention if need be, so that otherwise unsustainable standards of extravagance and opulence, and wasteful spending, may be enjoyed by the world's most prosperous people—and then only by the prosperous among them.

We can defend Salman Rushdie and Taslima Nasreen against government-sanctioned or government-permitted terrorism, but defence against savage or unprincipled international behaviour in the name of trade not only escapes the terrorist label, it is now dignified by the label of globalization of markets. As the terms and conditions of globalization are laid down by the west, it is, as ever, the western agenda, and not a broader human agenda, that is being pursued. It is one that defines modern as western, and assumes that all societies want to look, live and think like Europeans or North Americans. And many of the well-off in non-European societies are so indoctrinated by this assumption that they become enthusiastic collaborators and willing accomplices in a brand of fundamentalism which is as fanatic—because it is as non-negotiable—as the religious or ethnic variety. For those who are at the sacrificial end of globalization, it is not a new global era of mutual benefit and profit. For them it's more like on-going history—history as exclusion, as rejection, and as apartheid.

Until I became an adult, there was no such thing as human rights for any black person on earth. They were a monopoly of the west. It was difficult enough for others to be considered human, much less a human being with rights. In these circumstances it is extraordinary that the west makes human rights an article of foreign or trade policy, withholding or granting favours on the basis of a country's human rights record, when human rights are precisely what they have slaughtered for centuries, and which are under ruthless attack by western fundamentalism today in the policies which the powerful pursue against the powerless. America's sudden humanitarianism, and her current hard line on this issue, is particularly puzzling in the light of her own dismal record of staunch support even with lethal armaments to guarantee their survival—of one dictatorship after another. Democracy itself, not long ago, was dismissed as a utopian and unreliable idea for developing countries. Much better the military gang you could do business with and remote-control.

But the double standard is most shockingly demonstrated by the nuclear debate. Arsenals of nuclear weapons are still maintained by the nuclear powers who know they cannot use them against each other, since such a war would be total and unwinnable. No weapon is for use against an adversary who can match it. One must conclude that they are for use against the unarmed, to be kept in reserve as the ultimate weapon of terror, and used as and when mass genocide is judged necessary. Why else, instead of agreeing to eliminate these altogether, and calling for global disarmament, do the nuclear powers claim it their exclusive and perpetual right to stay nuclear, while they insist that the rest of the world disarm? Any formula that divides the world into nuclear and non-nuclear nations is as unrealizable as it is hypocritical. Without their total ban their spread cannot be stopped, and on what possible basis of moral superiority can their ownership be limited to a chosen few? The country now leading the campaign to prevent proliferation, and the dangers attending it, is the only country ever to have acted so dangerously as to use this weapon; and whose record in war besides includes more explosives dropped on the peasants of Indo-China than had been manufactured up to that time in history. A basic human right—the right to live without fear—is violated when such weapons exist in any hands at all.

The present freeze on fissile materials that America is now proposing was, in fact, originally proposed by the group of eight non-aligned countries at the United Nations as long ago as 1966, along with a comprehensive test ban, a gradual reduction of the stock of weapons, a ban on the use of nuclear weapons, and an assurance of security for non-nuclear states. None of this was acceptable at the time because it was part of the west's weapons bible to match weapon for weapon against other nuclear adversaries. The present partial change in attitude comes about because, according to defence analysts, the United States (and very likely, the other nuclear powers) have an abundance of fissile material and can afford a freeze on it. This would also make the American insistence on non-proliferation sound more plausible. Yet in this discriminatory context the Nuclear Non-Proliferation Treaty—as a substitute for global disarmament—sounds exactly like the Nazis making the Jews wear the Star of David, the easier to identify them for come what may.

I was wondering as I watched the 50th anniversary commemoration of the Auschwitz holocaust on TV earlier this year, what kind and amount of coverage the media would give to the 50th anniversary of Hiroshima and Nagasaki in August—when in hardly a second some 150,000 people were vaporized or burned to cinders, and some 100,000 subsequently died agonizing deaths from the effects of radiation. Fortunately the U.S. postal department seems to have abandoned its plan to issue postage stamps showing the destruction of the two cities with the caption that the atom bombs shortened the war. I don't know what kind of exhibition the Smithsonian Institution in Washington is putting on to commemorate the event, but Mr. Newt Gingrich has been reported as saying that ex-servicemen need have no fear, it will make Americans proud.

The point I am making is: that millions have not yet been accorded full human status. The Japanese in 1945 were not just the enemy. In a war where the mass slaughter of civilian populations was commonplace, they were singled out for apocalyptic punishment. It troubled no western conscience that they, being regarded as sub-human, could be made use of or as guinea pigs in an atomic experiment somewhat similarly, at the end of the Gulf War, American journalists hailed it as having been miraculously almost casualty-free. "No people were killed in this war," was their opinion. Apart from tens of thousands of troops pulverized in their trenches in 43 days of air war, there is no count of the massacres in residential areas, schools, hospitals and places of worship, or the famous bombing of the air raid shelter. But the talk-show journalists were right. No people were killed. These were not people. By the same token, sanctions can continue against Iraq (largely at America's insistence) to starve a population into submission.

It is the horror at the heart of every genre of terrorism, that it fails to recognize the other, whoever the other may be, as human. But an old and relentless refusal to do so creates the on-going aspect of terror I have talked about today.

One kind of fundamentalism generates another. The CIA's murder of Mossadeq, who challenged the writ of the oil giants in Iran, eventually gave rise to Ayatollah Khomeini. And this is a theme with historical variations over parts of the world. Societies strike back at what they see as re-colonization. In the process they destroy their own modern legacy along with what they target as westernization. So far as my own theme is concerned, perhaps the answer lies in an end to hegemonic ambition, whether political, cultural or economic, and the recognition of others as equals. Those who lead nations have to begin thinking along these lines.

The Myth Reincarnated*

On the subject of cartographies, new or old, and how a changing map of the world affects the concept of identity, the first question I have to ask myself is: What does what we call the world mean, and what is its validity for me? Has the prevailing wisdom about it been valid for me in the past? And is it any truer for me in the present?

To begin with, the world was flat and we would have fallen over the edge if we ventured too far. Then it became round. After that, once its shape was settled, its expanding size took over, and one's view of it, and of the forces of good and evil in it, was fashioned according to where one happened to be situated on the globe. What one perceived as civilization, and what as outer darkness, depended on one's location. Then came Europe's maritime age—those three hundred-odd years of European exploration, conquest, colonization and empire that were the forerunner of the world we now live in—when sea routes were opened by Europe for commercial traffic and the traffic was one-way. Those centuries established a lasting psycho-cartography of their own, positioning Europe and the Atlantic as fount and centre, and all the rest of the vastness of creation as outlying and peripheral, and created for the purpose of serving and servicing the centre. Areas were labelled Near, Middle or Far, depending on their distance from the centre and were judged by their usefulness to it. And this is how matters still stood when I was a child, growing up in a small town in north India, a town famous for landmarks that had figured in the *Ramayana*, beside a river that was sacred to mankind's oldest religion, in a countryside that was heir to a view of life unique for the immensity of its vision and the universality of its outlook. And so, of course, the prevailing wisdom not only had no validity for me, it was complete nonsense.

Yet this was the map of the world, and it was presided over by a breed of men who quite soberly assessed themselves as the rightful arbiters of affairs. The reigning reality divided the map into rulers and the

---

* Address at Conference on "New Cartographies: Commonwealth and Post-Colonial Literature," St. John's College, Oxford, 6 April 1995. Published in *Journal of Commonwealth Literature*, vol. XXX, No. 1, 1995.

lesser breeds they ruled. There was a master race and there were subject races—a term that was actually used by officialdom to define the larger part of humanity. Embedded and implicit in this scheme of things was a master civilization, Hellenic in origin; a master religion called Christianity, which was in fact a severely edited, sanitized, militarized and westernized version of an Asian religion and its scripture; a master philosophy which started with the Greeks, and from which all legitimate philosophical enquiry and scientific investigation must proceed, since progress, both as idea and development, was an achievement of the west. Following from these there was a master view of life, which was material, and an approach to phenomena that separated organic from inorganic matter, and split the human being into mind and body. All this fragmentation, compartmentalization, and irreconcilability, was enthroned as knowledge, and any other view of life was ignorance and monstrous superstition.

This western knowledge went into textbooks and was taught in schools, not as western knowledge but as Knowledge. It was the stuff of public policy and pronouncements, and of scientific articles. Fiction and cinema reflected its biases. A hero, by definition, could not be discovered to have one drop of oriental blood—unless that dark drop were found to be Spanish after all. And it was, of course, the standard by which art was judged. It even found its way into prayer. Above all it found its way into prayer, commandeering the kingdom of God as its exclusive monopoly.

Not one of its promoters and propagators dreamed that not one of these propositions would survive the re-drawing of the world's map and the surfacing of other points of view, because those who had thus arranged the world for their convenience, and laid down the laws by which alone it must be understood, had persuaded themselves not only of the everlastingness of their arrangement, but also of its inherent rightness. They saw it as part of the cosmic order, as natural and permanent as the solar system, and themselves as its God-appointed upholders. As late as 1936, the Dutch Governor-General of Indonesia made the remark: "We have ruled here for three hundred years with the whip and the club and we shall still be doing it in another three hundred years." As late as 1942, Winston Churchill declared he had not become His Majesty's First Minister in order to preside over the liquidation of the British Empire. He saw no such eventuality in sight, simply because any other order of things was quite unthinkable.

And yet, what was this fundamentalist imperial view but wishful thinking? And what could it lead to but more extreme wishful thinking on a more stupendous scale? For once that genie of land grab, that insatiable paranoia for power and glory, was out of the bottle, who could stop it, or tell where it would end? And if one myth had been such a roaring success, why not another? Where else, then, could all that myth-making lead but to the spawning of a master race within the master race, and a war to out-rival all wars, one that was based on the master myth that blue-eyed blonds had been born to conquer and rule the world? A myth, according to the dictionary, is "a purely fictitious narrative usually involving supernatural persons and embodying popular ideas on natural phenomena." And what have we had here on earth, under the cloak of recent, and not so recent history, but that?

I was brought up in an atmosphere of revolution, in a family committed to overturning the imperial order, so I grew up, as I said, believing that the reigning cartography and the doctrines enshrined in it had no more reality than the flat world we were going to fall off the edge of in earlier times, but it was in that colossal outer mythology that we were imprisoned, just as my parents and other patriots were locked up in jails for years of their lives. These people had no way of knowing when their ordeal, and the country's, would end, but they profoundly believed it must, because fictions must come to an end. One day, maybe not in their own lifetime, the distorted world would shift into perspective. Until then they would have to go on rejecting the evidence of solidity and permanence around them, and go on refusing to make terms with it, while they worked for the day when they would run their own lives, and speak for themselves from very different premises and assumptions. Looking back I am filled with wonder at the energy and optimism, but above all the sheer feat of imagination this must have taken, with words such as the Dutch Governor General's and Winston Churchill's in their ears, and the awe-inspiring structures of what looked like invincible power all around them.

The day did come. The maps that empires had brought into being were re-drawn. A host of countries came to be known as themselves and not as Europe's possessions. The west no longer had a monopoly of political significance. But the task of interpreting oneself in the postwar world ran into immediate and unanticipated hurdles. Let me give you a political example as it is an obvious one. It was the political scene in India that had been radically transformed by the transfer of power, so one hoped to be understood, first and foremost, in this context. My mother went as India's ambassador to the United States in 1949, two years after independence, to find that the world had once more been arbitrarily classified—by which philosopher I don't know—but this time into the First, Second and Third categories of a new moral order. My mother utterly failed, as did every Indian ambassador after her, to get the United States to understand India's refusal to line up with either of the two new military blocs, or to throw open the country to unbridled economic adventure either by her own or foreign entrepreneurs, preferring to follow a path of her own between capitalism and state socialism. It seemed the only map the United States recognize consisted of the reach and stretch of NATO and its other security alliances. This area with its bewildering array of dictatorships, theocracies and despotisms was for some reason known as the Free World, and anything that was not gung-ho capitalist was communist. We are all caught up in a particular time and place, and act in very different circumstances. India's was not an end-of-war awareness. It was a start-of-freedom awareness. It was the Indian ambassador's brief to convey her country's intention to chart a course of her own choosing, rather than follow the prescriptions of others, but this simple message was impossible to get across to a mentality that took as its starting point the proposition that inside of every human breast there was an American struggling to come out. Other points of view were regarded as treacherous betrayals. Over breakfast at his house one day, Mr. John Foster Dulles who was of a missionary frame of mind, gave my mother to understand that he had prayed for guidance on America's stand on the peace treaty with Japan, and he believed it had the Lord's sanction. It was the Indian ambassador's awkward task to tell him that in that case her Prime Minister was in disagreement with the Lord.

The Prime Minister made his first visit to America about that time, and was invited to dinner by leaders of industry. By way of introducing the company, and making the significance of the occasion clear, his host said, "Mr. Nehru, I want you to know there are X trillion dollars represented around this table." Nehru, who had not come begging for aid or bounty, and had never heard anyone introduced by the size of his bank account, was rendered temporarily speechless. And the failure of communication continued throughout the visit and for decades afterwards.

Interpretation in other areas was as frustrating. It seemed that authentic Indian music, dance or even a lecture had to be put through a trimming process to fit the fancies and attention span of its audience. The written word met somewhat the same fate. If it was not presented in the form of a puzzled outsider looking in, it had in any case to be a picturesque contrast to the western mainstream, and not a situation-in-itself that merited its own existence. Automatically much writing fell into this trap of attention-getting—as often it still does—measuring itself against the yardsticks of the west. To awaken awareness in an audience is hardly possible until one is fully self-aware. And I have often asked myself, are we still catering, seeing our selves through another's mirror, or have we come away at last, to act and not to react? I am not sure of the answer. Perhaps the answer would not matter if it did not affect a whole human canvas apart from writing.

I write novels with political settings. This was not a deliberate choice. Politics was all I had to work with, if I may use the word to signify a childhood filled with the sound and fury, and overflowing with the yearnings, of the national movement for independence, when all issues—from the cloth you wore to the food you ate and the company you kept—were political issues; when personal and political fates were inextricably bound, and political and social history merged with private lives. I could no more distance myself from that inheritance than a shoemaker's child can escape the smell of shoe leather. Why pin a novel to a political event, or a political vision, or its betrayal? Because it happened to be the outer focal point that stirred my imagination? It had nothing to do with politics as ideology or message, only with the strong and constant awareness I have had since birth, of a concept called India. My fiction was about a de-mythologized India whose people were much the same, as virtuous or as rascally, as anyone else. They had wanted to be free, and once free, they wanted to run their own lives. In the course of doing so the golden landscape of freedom decayed, power corrupted, and idealism became a ghost, but one that still haunted the house. None of this was exotic or mystifying. It was not picturesque or ethnic. It did not present a suitably modified version of a quaint colourful land of eastern intrigue and western example. It did not rise out of, or boil down to, the proverbial heat and dust seen through the lenses of the Raj or the after-Raj, because inside of me there was an Indian, buried for centuries, struggling to come out, looking and behaving like an ordinary human being. Because we had had no political voice, I found it especially satisfying to express myself politically and to speak a political idiom that was rootedly Indian, yet modern in its 20th century legacy. And it is no secret that India is the hub of my own inspirational universe. What I've tried to do is to discover the sort of behaviour politics and religion breed in the newly independent but ancient society we are.

Cartography turned another cartwheel when the disintegration of the Soviet Union brought another set of maps into being, and yet another moral order whose mantra was the market. An American academic told us that with communism collapsed, history was over. Since it had just re-started for some of us this sounded as peculiar as the Free World had, or the flat world before it, or the saga of the survival of the whitest that had once substituted for history. The collapse of Communism began to sound odder when democratic elections brought it back to power in several countries—so far as I can recall, in Bulgaria,

Lithuania, Mongolia and the former Yugoslav federation of Serbia and Montenegro. Even in Russia the Communists won 64 seats, just 10 less than Yeltsin's party. And to crown the whole paradox, the world's only Hindu kingdom, Nepal, elected a Communist government. Not to mention China, or that India till recently had three Communist State governments, one of which is heading for two decades in power. However, it seems to be the prevailing assessment that from now on markets will rule the world through a process known as globalization. The fact of advanced communications and floating populations, which either choose, or are driven by necessity, to live elsewhere, does give a superficial legitimacy to this idea. But globalization looks like the latest incarnation of a rugged old myth, in circumstances where essential power, in the shape of finance and industry, armaments and technology, is still controlled by the west, and the laws of the market divide us up as ever—like entry queues at airports—into sheep and goats, a nobility and a proletariat. From its dangerous trade policies that use Third World lands as dumping grounds for their toxic waste, and brook no interference in the capture of markets, to racist immigration policies, globalization looks like a master plan to the same old world. It gives us one more demonstration of that fundamentalist attitude which, since Christopher Columbus, has allowed for no alternative view of God or man.

As for identity, which flourished in the crucible of a fight for freedom, and fought back when it was under attack, now a fake connectedness sabotages the need for struggle. A sense of Indianness first took shape in response to British domination, and the British, like other, older encounters, also expanded and enriched Indian identity. But now as we are regimented and supervised into the images laid down by the managers of the global economy, and re-engineered to fit the culture of endless, mindless consumerism, we will be stripped of family, community, tradition and lose touch with the complex network of material, emotional and spiritual interdependence that goes into the making of a truly human society. All that is exceptional in us, by which we would evolve our own modern personality, will face extinction. Beneath the surface likenesses there will remain deep, unexplored sub-surfaces with agendas of their own, whole floating worlds beneath the ruling western agenda. Somewhere in space the dialogue between Mr. John Foster Dulles and my mother—as between the missionary and the heathen—will go on at cross purposes. Mr. Nehru will forever sit speechless with shock, encircled by American millionaires. And the uniqueness of India's identity will have to wait for another day to dawn.

As it always does, it will. Its reach and spread will not lie within the four corners of an ideology, or imperatives, conceived in, and laid down by the west. It will not be confined to an atomized, undernourished, obsessively individualistic consciousness. Nor will it be ruled by technology, biology, commerce and the like, though all these will be part of it. In a genuinely new era the very assumptions that have been taken for granted till now may have to change. It may be the East's turn to act as catalyst and agent of change in the modern western sensibility, as the west has been for us in the past. Until the white man puts down his burden, the re-drawing of maps alone cannot become the equalizing experience one naively supposed it would be. The world changes only as one's perception of it changes.

Some Thoughts on the Puzzle of Identity*

There is a meditation technique that takes the form of an enquiry. It is called Koham Dhyana, meaning who am I? This is an unravelling process directed inward from familiar labels like one's name, sex and nationality to the meaning of who, and why, one is—the idea being that true awareness is realized only when we shut out external stimuli, from the sights, sounds and smells that bombard us, to the historical and geographical factors that crowd in on us, and only through the discipline of letting go everything connected with the ego, until we come to the answer which is both deeply personal and universal. But as this ancient technique requires total silence, it may not be appropriate to try it here in place of this lecture. Failing this, there's only the outside world for answers, a poor substitute that has a way of partitioning and pigeonholing us rather than integrating us. Onc way to avoid being chopped up into bits might be simply to say: I'm a member of the human race and a citizen of the world, and leave it at that. But given the condition of the world the human race inhabits, with its blessings so unequally distributed and so undemocratically controlled, and ruled as it still is, by the perspective and priorities of those in power, this seems too general an answer—there being nothing much in common between citizens on one side of the globe and another. And then it is impossible to ignore all the ferocious wars of identity—national, racial, ethnic and religious—going on in this very world. And though this outer scaffolding does not determine all that we are, it is probably a useful place to start. So my own puzzle starts with India, and the fact that it was British India when I was born.

To put that environment into its historical perspective, it was an India which as a pre-industrial economy—till then a wealthy competitor in 18th century markets—had come under the control of a company of foreign merchants. This, followed by foreign political domination, was probably one of the most effective combinations of political power and vested interest that ever reduced a country to penury and a psyche to fracture. Even or perhaps especially, the benefits of empire—its roads, railways and telegraph wires for example—only made plunder of the

* The Ravenscroft Commonwealth Literature Lecture, University of Leeds, 18 February, 1993. Published in *Journal of Commonwealth Literature*.

land more efficient, while the people were only required to pay their rents and dues to their new landlords and keep their place in the feudal order. Unlike earlier landlords—Turks, Mughals and others who came to stay, be Indianized and absorbed into the bloodstream and the social fabric—the British chose to remain foreign and Olympian, supported by an elaborate, if unstated, system of segregation. There was an Indian society, and a white society, and no easy coming and going between them. As a child of parents involved in the national movement for independence I hardly ever saw the English and all I knew about them was that they were nervous of germs, and put something called antimacassar on their drawing room chairs. Also unlike earlier governments at Delhi, this one saw itself as a civilizing mission, so that a challenge to it was not just a traitorous offence, punished by imprisonment, exile or the gallows, it was an offence against the natural order of things, and the moral order of the universe. This, then, was the empire my parents were up against, paying for their opposition to it with long prison sentences and other forms of harassment, heartbreak and persecution, and one of them with his life.

Did this make snarling fanatics of them, wanting to tear every Englishman limb from limb? Actually, what it all boiled down to—apart from a refusal to tolerate British rule—was a passionate admiration for British qualities of character, lifelong friendships with English people, English governesses for us children, and custard pudding for dinner. Such are the intricacies of any encounter that is to any extent human, never mind what history, economics or statistics tell us, or what the rules lay down. The rules, of course, were there. There were railway compartments, park benches and clubs reserved For Europeans Only, and schools that admitted Indians but whose textbooks and curricula had no connection with India. On the silly side of arrogance the myth of British superiority made it obligatory for the English to mispronounce our names. They also called Asia the Near, Far or Middle East,—and they still do—depending on how near or far it was from Whitehall. And since their prestige had to be safeguarded, Charles Laughton as Henry VIII could not be shown gnawing at great hunks of meat at his dinner table. An English monarch could not in any case be shown eating with his fingers and the censors deleted this scene from the film for colonial viewing. No Englishwoman could be called "that woman" so the film, That Hamilton Woman, was re-titled Lady Hamilton. And love was a hopeless dilemma in the films and romances of the period if the English heroine discovered that the Englishman she had fallen in love with in some outpost of empire was suspected to have a drop of oriental blood. A tragic ending of suicide or renunciation could only be averted if the last chapter revealed that the drop of blood was Spanish. Years later when I watched Paul Scott's Jewel in the Crown I was shocked into remembering the atmosphere of crude white arrogance I had known as a child, one that made every nerve scream protest, as one lived out the hurts and humiliations, the furies and frustrations of trying to become merely visible in a Europe-dominated world, in a world where the west was The World, and the rest of humanity a fringe on its edges.

All this was bad enough without the people who couldn't pronounce our names becoming our interpreters and setting themselves up as intermediaries between us and everybody else. With the exception of those whose dedicated scholarship introduced the Sanskrit classics to the west, and others who became intimate with the splendours and problems of the land, the interpreters were usually the empire's standard bearers and saw India in its hallowed light, from Kipling's colourful stories to Winston Churchill's powerful prose. And like the textbooks I had at school, this inspired output had nothing much to do with India. Kipling's stories were about Europeans in the proverbial heat and dust of a dangerous land where the lesser breeds were wilfully hell-bent on obstructing the progress of empire, and good natives were the ones who showed a doglike devotion to the white man. Churchill's oratory referred to a patch of pink on the map belonging to His Majesty the King Emperor. And then there was the procession of visitors from Katherine Mayo to Beverly Nichols who between teatime and cocktails pronounced their own weighty little verdicts on India. The vocabulary of colonial discourse was stocked with heavy, rock-solid phrases such as "the subject races" and words like "heathen," which assumed a perfectly natural division of the world into rulers and ruled, and took for granted the power relationships of the time, of class, of colour and of race. Our interpreters actually spoke and wrote these words and phrases in all earnestness. The British Foreign Office drafted documents and conducted policy in this officials. Colonial literature and cinema grew out of them, portraying a Never Never Land of horrid eastern villainy and handsome western virtue. In the film called Gunga Din, Douglas Fairbanks Jr. and Cary Grant battled heroically with a band of Indian thugs led by a wicked old thug made up to resemble Mahatma Gandhi. And Indian news reached the outside world suitably selected and doctored by the Government. Mass upsurges became "unrest," and could take second place to important items such as the fact that the Maharaja of Mysore had shot a 900-lb. tiger. The interpreters added their own hardy building blocks to this edifice of imperial language. Immortal among these are Kipling's description of the lesser breeds as "half devil and half child" and Churchill's divinely ordained "mission of Christendom" and "the mission of the English-speaking peoples."

The mythology of empire created by this language dies hard, which may explain the long-lasting Raj nostalgia, whereas nobody has given a second thought to the Dutch or Portuguese empires which had no comparable supporting mystique, and remained brisk, businesslike affairs of conquest and profit. They had nothing resembling Land of Hope and Glory, that emotive combination of hymn and battle cry, glorifying conquest and sanctifying occupation with God's blessing. Imperial language regarded Christianity and Christian scripture as its indispensable ally, God had a starring role in the whole enterprise, and it was Christian soldiers who marched to extend the frontiers of empire. Thus we were reduced by this language to figments of the Anglo-Saxon imagination. Even a child felt harrowed and puzzled by it, up against a mythical orient created by the writers, historians and other upholders of the Raj. Which was real, I kept asking myself, me or they, for it was clear that we both could not be.

It is the triumph of any mystique that it looks as if it partakes of eternity, that it is as undeniable and elemental as a fact of nature—whether it is the feminine mystique or empire—when of course it is nothing of the kind, and only needs a different arrangement of words on a page to start undoing it, along with all the images and stereotypes it invented. And the British empire began to be undone as words began to be differently arranged on a page, taking us out of the stranglehold of the imperial point of view. After independence the intermediary was eliminated, and Churchill's "mission of the English-speaking peoples" became the radically different mission of people of all climes and colours who had made English their own. And Europe has now recognized this development, and rewarded it with last year's Nobel Prize for Literature, and with the Peace Prize, to representatives of people colonized and dispossessed by the white man. It is a long way from Kipling to Derek Walcott and Rigoberta Menchu, and one might say the wheel has come full circle, but has it? How much difference can prizes make to the great structures of power that still control us? Or the kind of people we have become as the result of a particular past? There *is* a post-modern east, but some of its best and worst features mirror the post- modern west.

Let's take the East-West encounter, as this collision of cultures, this seizure of land and resources, and establishment of hegemony, and deprival of dignity is called. It is still a fact of our life, our politics, our character, our literature, as anything that happens to one continues to be. We are indelibly shaped by it. We are still maimed and scarred by it, aroused to anger, admiration, or imitation by it. It remains an ineradicable experience, and our most recent frame of reference. The complexity of this (or probably any) encounter lies in the fact that it was not all of a piece. The responses to it were many and various. Some gave their lives to the struggle for freedom from British rule; others supported and served the Raj and reaped the knighthoods and rewards of its loyal servants; for the majority it may well have been one more experience of new masters, this time under a more crushing burden of exploitation. And it was not all of a piece even for an individual. Love and hate, opposition and friendship, rejection and adoption could all engage the same human heart. The British added one more complex layer to Indian identity and we are still sorting out the fallout of this last top layer.

But who, really, are "we"? At one end of the spectrum is a majority who still cannot write, and have yet to write their experience. So present writing may well be an elite rehearsal for the more representative performance yet to come once *these* Indians—which means *most* Indians—can express themselves directly. Their expression will be less allied to western taste, patronage and publication, and it may reveal an identity very different from the one we fancy ourselves as having today. Over four decades of universal suffrage have made this grassroots identity very decisive and tumultuous in the political process, but it still has to surface in literature. At the other end of the spectrum are the very rich, who for all practical purposes have seceded from India, even if they remain in India as Indian nationals. As far as their goals, their interests, and even their material arrangements are concerned, they have pulled out, and have much less to do with India than with their counterparts in the west. And the implications of the social and economic fragmentation this has brought about are as devastating in their impact on the country as of those who want India's boundaries re-drawn. India's two economies, the vulgar ostentation and growing consumerism on the one hand, and a continuing and even growing impoverishment on the other, are a sign of the complete separation between the rich and the poor. It used to be said the poor had no nation. They have been, and still are, lured or dragged across continents to provide labour. Now it is the rich who have no nation and no loyalty, except to money.

In between these two extremes lies an India where the very meaning of "India" is now the cause of slaughter and debate, and where the assertion of identity is taking the form of demands for greater autonomy, or outright secession from the Union, some fuelled by Muslim or Sikh religious fundamentalism, while Hindu fundamentalism wants to preserve unity by bottling and pickling India in an exclusive Hindu mould and clamping it into a fixed unchanging identity. To start conceiving India as the cultural monopoly of Hindus, with every other culture on Indian soil seen as an imposter and outsider, would not only be a radical departure from the cardinal principles that went into the making of modern India, but a misrepresentation of Indian history, and an abuse of cultural memory. It would result in a shrunken, artificial self-image made up of selected racial memories. It would deal a death blow to my own cherished sense of Indianness, whose very essence is its ethnic and religious diversity, and its cultural plurality. But this is the kind of death-blow many like myself are now facing in India, with mystical dreams and blood urges dictating what nationality should mean.

It I may give a personal illustration, I cannot help being acutely aware of the danger of this lethal combination of nationalism and religion, for it has blown two members of my own family to shreds, leaving almost nothing of their mortal remains to cremate at their state funerals.

Then there are the writers, those who explain us to ourselves and to the world. Many of those who write in English live and write in the west. They are not affected by the raw winds assailing India or—which is more crucial—by the texture of daily life. They are not encumbered by the nitty gritty of carving out a continuity from difficult, sometimes unpredictable circumstances, with gaining an inch of breathing space at a time in the on-going process of building a nation that has only in recent times become a nation. They live in circumstances so materially and psychologically removed from those of their countrymen on the subcontinent as to give them almost nothing in common—least of all an identity—connected with hailing from the same piece of territory on a map. They are reacting to the pressures and concerns of an environment that is not Indian, and are fashioning identities born of choice, not of history.

And then, who we are, is further complicated by the fact that the west is still The World, and we are more shadow than substance in conditions where the west dominates industry and capital, technology, finance, information and trade; where no sovereign authority is allowed to interfere with the laws or the lawlessness of the market; and with the collapse of the Soviet Union there is now no countervailing ideology in politics or economics to act as a brake on it. It used to be the empire that told us who we were. Now it is this new empire, of managers of the global economy, who warn us we will have no existence unless we toe the line, while the marketers of images tell us we have no identity but the one they choose to impose on us. At another level, literature, like everything else in this post-modern age, toes the line too when the deconstructionists tell us the same thing, that interpretation is the experience, that every written word and sentence has to be decoded, and has no existence unless it is decoded. And perhaps this would distort us less if all decoding did not proceed from European insights, European cultural traditions, and European approaches to rationality and logic.

Few things have been more destabilizing for millions of people across the globe and for their concept of identity than this imperialism in a new garb. It axes the roots, and cuts off the blood supply, of ancient systems of thought, of the oldest values known to mankind—of community, sharing, and concern for the weak and vulnerable. It rides roughshod over a view of life older then the hills whose health and harmony depended on taking the whole universe outside oneself into consideration. These are cultural values that were first threatened during the era of colonial domination, when they began to be challenged through processes of development and modernization which, in effect, meant westernization. "Do like we do," the west declares, "and you'll be rich like us." So *Rich Like Us* was the title I gave to a novel of mine in which a fizzy drink called Happyrola allies itself with local corruption and a dynastic dictatorship to launch India into modern times. The west's is still the dominant and domineering culture. The world is still seen through its cultural lenses, analyzed through its modes of thought, and prescribed the remedies Europe thinks best. Imposing the western agenda has often meant psychological disorientation, physical dislocation and political tumult as systems alien to the west struggle to provide goods they cannot possibly provide, for people who cannot afford to buy them and would not know how to use them. The result has been enrichment at one end and abysmal poverty at the other. An all-powerful market that allows nothing to stand in the way of its access to commodities that will maintain the lifestyle of the world's most privileged people has thought nothing of going to total war for the purpose, as it did in the Gulf most recently. Its capture of forests and minerals and other natural resources has forced people to migrate to already overburdened cities, and once their resource base and all their familiar comforting patterns of life and relationship are wrenched away, and their notions of identity thrown into a flat spin, has made them recruits for whatever illusory identities are on offer, or those rooted in a mythical or nonsensical past, or simply in criminality and mafiadom. And the fact that this kind of volcanic upheaval is on, must make all talk of identity in a lecture hall, or discussion about it at literary conferences, as far removed from what is actually happening as Marie Antoinette's hair style from the business end of a guillotine. But that kind of yawning chasm is frequently present in situations where the Book, the text, the theory, take precedence over life and humanity, and when high priests act as intermediaries between man and his salvation, especially when the high priests are grafting their own somewhat blinkered vision on it.

It could be this ruthless encroaching tide of alien values that helps tip cultures backwards into the cauldron of fundamentalism, in order to resist it, and save themselves from being bulldozed in a direction they don't want to go. When they think about the centuries of Christian power and the disasters that Christianity, as interpreted by the west, have visited on mankind, from crusades and genocides, to the millions of corpses piled up in two major and countless minor wars, they may not think it a very good idea to make themselves in the western image, apart from their objections to what the west regards as worthwhile personal goals. This veritable onslaught of a western lifestyle may be helping to breed a nostalgia for a past that may well be mythical, but is no less powerful on that account. It may be helping to drive societies back to a way of life, good or bad, but rooted in their own history; or goading groups within societies to aggrandize religion, or to seek refuge in smaller sub-national identities—all of which may be remedies much worse than the disease they are fleeing from, but do look like havens in a storm. Ironically enough, the multiculturist policy in Britain which seeks in good faith to understand and accommodate other cultures, sometimes ends up supporting the obscurantist elements of those cultures, and encourages pockets of medievalism whose spokesmen and defenders are men, leaving women to start their struggles for freedom from scratch and not allowing them to routinely benefit from the liberal social environment they are living in. In this respect the multiculturist policy resembles our imperial interpreters who used to promote the archaic, the quaint and the exotic as the genuine article and true representative of a culture, when true tradition is not static, but something we make and unmake by our sweat and toil as we go along.

I confess I am ill-equipped by background and temperament to appreciate the world of modern-day no-holds-barred capitalism assisted by rapidly changing technology, having been brought up to the view that a politics or an economics, a private or a public life motivated solely by self-interest and self-satisfaction was one that could only degenerate into greed, grab and lunacy. I grew up, of course, in rare times, as any atmosphere created by the striving for freedom always is. I realize that ordinary life does not often breed or sustain such an atmosphere. My own novels are about how the idealism of an emergent nation has withered and rotted in corruption and decay. But I am tainted by those rarefied times and cannot shed them any more than I can my skin, and so I hobble about some areas of the post-modern world, this world they tell me is the real world, which somehow looks strangely unreal to me. Oh, I can see it is there. What I want to know is, is it true? I have to keep asking myself as I did in childhood of the solid, undeniable empire that surrounded, pervaded and ruled us, is *it* real, or am I, because we both cannot be. So when they tell me what I see around me is the new reality we must accept and pay homage to, I've heard that story before. Believe it, they say, the old ideas have been overthrown, there is no scheme of things but this. Fit into it or die. But for me it is the old tricky question of illusion and reality once again. Seeing is not always believing, and very far from accepting. I know the landscape flashing past is really standing still, and that my own reckoning has to be with its eternities, and not with the brute, literal fact that I am being propelled past it, rushed in a direction I don't want to travel.

Anyway, I ask myself, how is this direction they want to rush me in any different from all the rampaging fundamentalisms that are tearing sanity to bits? Isn't this inflexible, intractable western grip on the world with its well-intentioned diktat: Be reasonable, do it my way; or: Do like we do and you'll be rich like us; isn't this a form of fundamentalism that non-westerners have been facing since Christopher Columbus, when life on the planet began to be savagely, or benevolently, but in any case, methodically refashioned in the western image? Haven't we lived in the fundamentalist climate of the west's own non-negotiable revelations of the truth? One of these, Communism, they say for some reason is now "over." The other which they call economic know-how and the supremacy of the market, is now supposed to be the road to salvation. Yet it hasn't even the grace of the old imperialism, for the old imperialist was on the spot. He had responsibilities to fulfil, he was accountable to his Parliament. He was a human being whose face we saw and whom we dealt with at a hundred human levels, with all the give and take that involved, albeit as unequals. The new imperialism is an absentee push-button affair and involves no human process at all, only profits.

Of course I'm slow to understand the advantages of this New Age, from its political and economic priorities to the marvels of its technology. In an age of expertise I'm not an expert on anything and I know nothing about the formulae that make the world go round. I've opted out of the latest model, whatever it might be. I try never to be in fashion. I'm so untrendy I even live in India, instead of somewhere more congenial where things work, and creature comforts are not in short supply. I don't write about caste, joint family, or picturesque ethnicity. I'm more interested in trying to trace in human terms the implications of what happens to us politically, the ideas and behaviour that religion breeds in us, and my on-going character has been India. I've never used an electric typewriter, because where I live the electricity is apt to be cut off in the middle of a sentence for a couple of hours. Nor do I use a word processor. I've always believed words were processed in a cavern in one's brain, and flowed on to paper straight from there. My town hasn't caught up with the communications revolution and my telephone does me a favour when it works, so it was quite a feat serving on the jury of the Commonwealth Writers' Prize for two years, and keeping in close touch with the judging centres at Sydney and Toronto. So I'm the last person who should be talking to you about the times we live in. A couple of years ago at a literary conference in Hongkong where writers talked about their methods of composing, a young Welsh poet said that word processors were such a remarkable invention that he even found his style changing when he started to use one. But as I plan to stick to my style, this decided me finally against ever using one. And as to methods of composing, I doubt I'll ever find one as good as staring out of the window. I'm backward in other ways, too. I feel dreadfully out of step with the times when I come across thousand-page novels or somebody's life in six volumes. I don't buy them because I can't stagger home with them, or relax in bed with them, but also because floods of words, like affluence beyond a point, or speed beyond a point, leave me stunned and stupid. It may also be that I have a natural bent for brevity and for leaving *out* as much as I can. It may be my way of countering the explosion of verbiage that has hit us, and the fact that pause, silence and emptiness are so little valued for the power they possess. The best thing about a novel used to be that no one had to read it. It might be something one discovered on a bookshelf all by oneself, a treasure awaiting discovery, perhaps long after it was written. But now, the publicity, the hype, the commerce surrounding it are so relentless, that this most magical way of passing one's time has been relegated like all else—like music, art and sport—to merchandise, and ourselves to one more form of bombardment.

I'm also bewildered by all the intimidating theories about writing. I can see the point of analyzing the physical world. Put a cross-section of a leaf or a frog under a microscope and you've found out something about it that will hold good six months hence. But that's because they're dead. The writer who is cross-sectioned and analyzed is not only still around, she's also changing. And writing is in part a mysterious process that must needs remain mysterious. In any event it's a risky business, and a thankless job, being an intermediary, as I'm sure the Pope must have discovered when the Reformation began. And I've wondered if this extent of dissection of texts doesn't make writers, readers and reviewers self-conscious? Just as the Welsh poet's computer was spawning a new style, are the critics and analysts spawning style? Do readers crouch in wait for hidden meanings, and writers labour to supply ever more "special effects"? The truth may be far more simple, far less contorted and acrobatic. Yet the whole business of making sense of anything seems to have passed into a maze from which it will never emerge. Instead of saying: Row, row, row your boat gently down the stream, we seem to be saying: Propel, propel, propel your craft languidly down the liquid solution. And at the end of all these contortions the experts seem to have come up with the melancholy conclusion that we are spinning without a centre, that in this post-modern era there is no fixed meaning to anything since everything, including identity, keeps changing, and every shift is subject to many interpretations.

Another thing I can't seem to catch up with is the vogue for telling it all. We are repeatedly reminded—in case we may have forgotten-of the behaviour of bodies in bed. Now I think what is being celebrated by all this compulsive repetition and description, in books and cinema, is possibly the re-discovery by Christians that there's no such thing as original sin. And of course that's great news. But the Renaissance celebrated it so much more interestingly. It produced not only a wealth of magnificent nudes, but a wealth of investigation into scientific and natural phenomena, in short an expansion of knowledge and the whole human consciousness, which resulted in a new way of looking at life. This time round the celebration seems to be stuck with coitus and climax. But maybe this has something to do with the word processor.

To go on with my misfit condition, I have trouble convincing myself that the all-powerful market will bring us to the promised land of prosperity, since even in Toronto a year ago—which is one of the world's wealthiest cities—I had only to walk out of the plush hotel I was put up in, to see a line of beggars in rags holding out their hats for coins. Yet it seems to me as foolish to say that capitalism has failed because I saw beggars in Toronto, and see them here in Britain, as that communism has failed. No system that succeeded in educating millions, compressing centuries of growth into a quarter century, and fiercely defending its soil in a world war as Communism did, can be said to have failed. What has failed is the capacity of these two western gospels to understand and make room for each other, and profit by an intelligent combination of the two. Why should it be impossible for people to take the best of all human experience—this common human ancestor—into their blueprints for the future?

When I hear that communism is "over," as many say that religion is "over," I wonder if anything can be over that has once happened to us, and has jerked or stretched our awareness to the smallest degree? I am not a Communist or any other ist, but I do know what it did for a society like India—and probably for the world—was serve as a conscience-awakener. If communism triumphed at all, it is because it would have taken another hundred years for any other idea to break through the bastions of caste, class and privilege. Here's what the words "You have nothing to lose but your chains" did for a character named Sonali in my novel *Rich Like Us.* And I quote:

> I wrote that sentence in large capitals in one of my notebooks to keep its lilting promise before me. Why had nobody, nobody at all, put those words together in exactly this eight-word formation before? . . . It unlocked a small high window in my mind, an unused attic window, and air rushed in to swirl old scraps and particles around in a blizzard of dust, settling them after the storm in strange new configurations. . . . A sightless beggar reflected in the glass show window of a shop displaying highheeled snakeskin shoes. Baby brides taking their dolls with them to their husbands' homes. My attic window gave me an anguished awareness I would never have had, though all that I became aware of at one stroke had been as if forever present in my consciousness.

What more is there to say except that it is through this deepening, expanding, metamorphosing consciousness that identity takes a beating, or blossoms, and is perpetually renewed and reshaped. Through this open awareness historians re-interpret history and people everywhere continually re-invent themselves. We are not what we were yesterday, or what we will be tomorrow. But our intelligent recycling of whatever happens to us, the human race—either individually or collectively—can help us transcend even the most brutal and agonizing of these experiences, and transform them into patterns ever more human and humane. As I wrote this a literary example came to mind, Ishiguro's novel *The End of the Day.* When I read this I thought how seamless an example of interwoven identities it was; how identity in this case had resolved itself flawlessly through art; how British, and yet how exquisitely noiseless and Japanese a novel it was; and with so perfect an end-product, how utterly irrelevant was the question of Ishiguro's identity.

As an Indian I am a mix of cultures and influences, of Hinduism, Islam and Christianity, of east and west. The interplay of a variety of historical and educational factors in my upbringing should perhaps have torn me apart, made me unsure of my identity, and driven me to seek some simple answer to the question: who am I? Curiously enough it has had the opposite effect. I have learned to make the most of my cultural confusion and to regard it as a blessing, not a curse. The act of writing has given me, besides, the opportunity to look critically at some of the formidable bastions of identity we base our lives on—nation, class, family. I have had occasion to publicly oppose the dynastic ambition of my family, and the brief dictatorship over which it presided, and to discover that the labels others know us by are not what we are. I've come to understand that what I am instead, is a writer. Any narrower identity separate from writing gradually disappears into the words one puts on a page, until eventually "writer" is the only nametag that fits. A woman, an Indian, a citizen of the world—in the course of a lifetime one is many things—but not until I had shaken off the labels others had given me, become a cheerful traitor to my origins, unlearned much I had been taught, and put experience together quite differently in words on a page, did I know who I was.

To get back to the meditation technique I began with, one is born, according to the Hindus, in order to realize oneself. The sages did not mean the writing process, but perhaps there's no better way to make a start.

I don't know about you, but I'm not spinning without a centre. Nor do I feel there is no sense to be made of anything because the centre does not hold. Mine holds, maybe because I am not in the state of advanced modernity categorized as post-modern. I'm not European, and so I don't have to go by Europe's categories, or squash myself into Europe's conceptual and cultural scheme of things, its bare minimum field of facts and data accessible to scientific research, its dependence on the material for explanations, its gung-ho physical emphasis. There are other ideas and approaches that merit study in their own right. There is a whole other universe of value waiting to come to light which does not lend itself to definition in European terms, or *on* European terms. And it will, the day the white man lays down his burden, and holds out his hand in equal partnership. For it is too diverse a world for one angle of vision to explain it, and one set of conclusions to decide how it should be run. There must be creative compromises possible between here and now and the hereafter. It may be time for the *west* to strike it rich by acknowledging other angles of vision, and by using other keys to open up its own culture to new definition. Quite a lot—including its own construct of post-modern identity—that reduced and under-nourished consciousness which plays second fiddle to technology, biology, chemistry, commerce and manufacture—may begin to be sorted out in the process. Only in the give and take of a more egalitarian climate can we begin gratefully to recognize what we owe each other, and only then can we justly celebrate our combined, stupendous human heritage, and partake of a truly common identity.

The Schizophrenic Imagination*

I am a little dazzled, and more than a little intimidated, by all the scholarship I have heard propounded in the last few days. I have also wondered when "post-colonial" is supposed to end. First we were colonials, and now we seem to be post-colonials. So is "colonial" the new Anno Domini from which events are to be everlastingly measured? My own awareness as a writer reaches back to x-thousand B.C., at the very end of which measureless timeless time the British came, and stayed, and left. And now they're gone, and their residue is simply one more layer added to the layer upon layer of Indian consciousness. Just one more.

The title of my talk may be misleading in terms of studies made about the subject—of which I know nothing. So let me begin by explaining that I am thinking of schizophrenia as a state of mind and feeling that is firmly rooted in a particular subsoil, but above ground has a more fluid identity that doesn't fit comfortably into any single mould. A schizophrenic of this description is a migrant who may never have left his people or his soil. We are all somewhat divided selves, but I'm referring to the divisions that history and circumstance impose on the complex creatures we already are. Let me take the example of Jawaharlal Nehru, a product of colonial times who called himself a man of two worlds, but unlike the quotation describing one of these as dead, the other powerless to be born, both his worlds were alive and vigorous. He was not in any limbo. That was the trouble. His was a life lived in two-plus-one cultures, in many ways a story of assimilation, yet the times he lived in and the role he played in them placed his cultures in conflict and confrontation. The struggle for independence gave the conflict a historic setting, and his life and personality a very different direction from the one it would otherwise have taken.

Educated Indians had, of course, been in contact with western civilization since the British occupation, though most Indians, who lived

---

* Plenary Address at ACLALS Conference, University of Kent, Canterbury, 30 August 1989. Published in *Wasafiri*, No. 11, Spring 1990 and in *Unbecoming Daughter of the Empire*, Dangaroo Press, 1993.

by the sun, the rain and the seasons were not touched by it. But many of the educated, too, were affected only in their outer lives. It had not become second nature except for those few whose class and opportunities made this possible. Of these, some related to the East-West encounter by discarding their Indians to become brown carriers of the white culture they admired and adopted. But nationalism produced another breed of westernized Indian for whom his plural culture meant a bewildering reckoning with himself, a balancing act, where the priorities were never in doubt, but where "Who am I?" remained an on-going search and question. Nehru was one such Indian, and it may be that many of his countrymen and women are still sorting out the meaning of this particular historical experience.

In contrast, Nirad Chaudhuri, a man of the same generation as Nehru, born when the words empire and colonial still had benign associations, seems not only an unanguished product of the same period, but one who became a philosophical observer and erudite chronicler of the colonial framework he was born and bred in. After independence, at an advanced age, when few people emigrate of choice to set up house and put down roots somewhere else, he could leave India never to return, and could flourish heart-whole in what perhaps was, and is, the real country of his imagination, teaching the English how to stay English. For those who did not cross swords with the imperial order, it was simply the order of the day. For many it had a mystique, the elemental rightness, and right to be there, of a natural phenomenon.

A strong element of mystique attached to Nehru's outlook too, but it was the mystique of the fight for freedom, though that is not all it was. It was also traceable to his peculiar involvement with India, as fact, as dream, and as possibility. He wrote in *Discovery of India*: "For we are very old, and trackless centuries whisper in our ears." He was aware of that whisper. One incident toward the end of his life sums up the quality of his involvement. The family was at the breakfast table. A nephew said the country was in a mess, its problems would never be solved, and he, for one, was getting out to settle abroad. Nehru's daughter was listening sympathetically. Suddenly Nehru who had remained silent, spoke in a rage, "Go where you like, but if I am born a thousand times, a thousand times I will be born an Indian." It was a statement of almost mystical emotion and power. It had an echo of the cult of the motherland, for in the early years of this century these had been the last words of more than one Indian martyr after he mounted the gallows for his execution. This was Nehru's subsoil speaking though he was a man deeply identified with other nationalisms, as also with the science, learning and pleasures of the west, and was better known as an internationalist than perhaps any other figure of his time. He was also saying that to transform your society, you have to be in it. The ultimate battles, whether for freedom or after it, are fought on your own soil. He was implying "My life is my message" as opposed to "My text is my message." But the impassioned ingredient in his makeup is common to those everywhere—from rebels against empire to iconoclasts in art and literature—who see that there are facts which must be denied, and that there is more than one way of looking at the world.

There is a story from the imperial era about an Englishman whose posting in the Sudan was over. He was to leave with his family for England and he was pleased when his little son begged to be taken to say goodbye to the statue of Gordon. The father was proud that his child remembered all he had been taught about General Gordon's magnificent defence of Khartoum, a heroic event in the annals of empire, and was deeply moved when tears ran down the child's face as they stood at the famous equestrian statue, until the boy asked, "Daddy, who's that man sitting on Gordon?" It is those who in all honesty and earnestness are looking at the horse and not the rider, who can fit neatly into no tradition except one that is in the making. If anyone wants to fit me into a tradition, it is this tradition-in-the-making they will have to settle for.

My own divided experience starts with belonging to North India, a region that has been spared no convulsion or folk experience, from epic marvels and a matchless metaphysics to repeated invasion and slaughter. My part of the Ganges plain is the cradle of Hinduism but it is home to Islam as well, and Indo-English by virtue of the continuing impact and fall-out of British rule. All three influences meet in the city of my birth whose original name, Prayag, figures in the *Ramayana*, while its present name, Allahabad, testifies to Muslim conquest and rule, and where every road in my childhood was named after an Englishman, the public park had a statue of stout old Queen Victoria, and down the road from our house two nights a week came dance music from a club that did not admit Indians.

Going to school was like arriving at the club that didn't admit Indians. My school admitted Indians but ignored India. As I was quite sure that India existed, I didn't place much faith in school. At home I was nourished on revolt. My elders were committed to rooting out foreign rule and had made a personal beginning by giving up their scholarship and their careers at the Bar to devote their lives and all their resources to the struggle for freedom. They were so enthralled with organizing for it, and being imprisoned for it, that I thought going to jail was a career. They had no regular incomes because they had given up their means of livelihood, but they found it so exhilarating doing without the comforts, amenities and certainties other people took for granted, that when I was introduced to what is known as normal life after independence, it gave me quite a shock with its very different priorities. I had never before met people who earned livings, took holidays, joined clubs, went shopping, and knew what tomorrow would bring, and they struck me as a quaint and exotic species. Above all, the whole business of entertaining, of serving elaborate meals to other well-fed people, and then going to *their* houses to be fed elaborate meals by *them*, seemed to me an extremely curious way of spending time. There are several aspects of normal life I still haven't got used to. I think I started to write books as a retreat from it. I know I am ill-equipped to be part of normal life. I will forever be an outsider looking in through its windows, marvelling at the sequences and continuities of normal life. When I try to read them, they look like hieroglyphics, a fascinating language for which I lack the code.

In a childhood filled with the sights, sounds and folklore, and sometimes the furore, of the national movement, nothing estranged me from school more than the way history was taught. Its content and perspective were so different from what I learned at home that I soon put school history in the same category as Kipling's Gunga Din—a rousing, rollicking white man's fable that had everything to do with the conqueror's image of the bullied, beaten Indian, loyal to his last gasp, and nothing to do with India. In short I didn't believe a word of it. I was also surprised to learn that ancient times began with Greece, that the world had been created in six days, and that all of religion was down in one little book. Though the nuns did their best with me, privately I suspected that God Almighty was my grandfather, and Jesus Christ must be my uncle, since he carried other people's sorrows on his back; that they, together with my father and mother, were special shining beings, and that the fight for freedom was the path to the Holy Grail. I knew I inhabited a huger, older universe of which school taught me only a meagre slice, yet paradoxically this little scrap filled the textbooks and ruled the world.

Home had its paradoxes, too, but they fell into place as part of a larger purpose. I can see my frail, spectacled, widowed grandmother sitting cross-legged on her bedroom floor reading in a low mutter from her enormous large-print *Ramayana*, and shrieking for a servant when a mouse darts across the floor, but she's the same woman who picketed foreign cloth shops not long before, and who once stayed firmly put at the head of a procession halted by the police. Let me quote what happened next from a written account. She was "knocked down . . . and hit repeatedly on the head with canes. Blood came out of an open wound in her head; she fainted and lay on the roadside." Within these outer tensions there were inner tensions, for non-violence does not come naturally to the human race, and my father once got solitary confinement for knocking down a jail guard who insulted my grandmother when she visited him in jail. I used to wish the time would come when my parents would stay home like other parents. For one of them the time never came, for my father died of his last imprisonment. I'm not sure whether a childhood lived in this heightened state of national and world awareness was euphoric or wretched. It is probably best described by Pushkin's reaction when he read Gogol's *Dead Souls*. After laughing uproariously all the way through it, he exclaimed, "Oh God, how sad our Russia is!" It has been said that a person who survives her childhood has enough information to last her for the rest of her days, and it must be true, or my novels would not have reflected the political idealism of an emergent nation, and its progressive destruction and decay. There is always an obstinate idealist hanging around in my fiction, usually with as much chance of success or survival as a snowball in Hades.

I did not set out to write "political fiction." I have no ideology except a vague sort that feels uncomfortable with title and privilege, with kings, queens and political dynasties. I have no message either, unless it is the non-message that Europe is not the centre of the world. Politics for me was an environment in which every issue was a political issue, and personal and political fates were inextricably bound. If it has remained a continuing awareness, it is because I live in an unsettled order, one I am trying to change, one where I am witness to the public and domestic misuses of power. And politics was for so long dictated by other people's view of us, that I have found it satisfying to give it Indian expression and interpretation. Yet though I use a political backdrop or events—since these happen to be the outer focal points that trigger my imagination, and also because I think we gain or lose significance in our relationship to events—I prefer to think of my fiction as having a sense of history, in a country where race, religion or caste can decide the course of a love affair, where it can take as much raw courage to choose a husband, or leave him, as to face a firing squad. The nuclear family with its attendant traumas is not for us. Our traumas like our families are built on a grander scale. From where I stand, looking at the horse and not the rider, it doesn't seem to me there *is* such a thing as a purely individual predicament. Too many other factors blur and burden it, including the weather. Fornication and adultery go on in India as anywhere else, but I'm not sure they can be given such free rein as in western fiction without becoming unrelated to a social condition where the individual is tied hand and foot, and often back-breakingly, to wider responsibility. For one thing he hasn't got the time. And she has even less. But as we approach western living conditions—as in my novel after next—there will be more time for adultery.

Then, societies that have lived long under foreign domination bring their own behaviour characteristics into play. Passivity can become an active choice, a strength, among people where invasion and re-conquest have been the pattern, because it is one's best chance of remaining whole. Sycophancy, too, is the hallmark of the survivor and all cultures have sycophants. But when I wonder why *we* produce them in such abundance—and this struck me strongly during the 1975-77 dictatorship known as the Emergency—then I have to ask, as I did in my novel *Rich Like Us*, whether Hinduism inclines a whole society to the status quo. Does it put out the fires of rebellion? Does it incline women to victimization, to individual and mass acts of horrifying self-sacrifice? Has the cult of virtue (female) and honour (male) been so ferocious and merciless in any other society that prides itself on its humane values? How do we explain this aspect of ourselves? I have been much preoccupied with the effects of Hinduism on character in my novels.

All Indians are not Hindus but all Indians must reckon with Hinduism since it is the dominant setting, the social and psychological atmosphere. Yet what it is we are reckoning with is hard to say when Hinduism has no beginning, no founder, no church, no commandments, no single bible, no single prophet or messiah. There can never be a law of blasphemy against Hinduism, or any other concrete religious measure to bring all Hindus into line. But memory and imagination are much the most powerful of human possessions, and give us almost unlimited scope for both enlightenment and bigotry. This, then, is the sky I and my characters live under, and in one sense I am nothing if I am not a Hindu. On the Indian subcontinent there is no escape from the aspect of cultural behaviour we call religious.

Some Hindus solve their problem of how to come to terms with Hinduism by dumping it and calling themselves atheists, agnostics, or secular. But this is no solution for a writer. If I change my name today to Henrietta von Blinkenstaff, who am I trying to fool? Can I quick-change my bones, my myths, or my grandparents? Can I forget that my great-grandmother became a suttee? So I find it more useful to say, Believe it, you are a Hindu. Now figure out, if you can, what that means, and fiction is part of the process of figuring it out. Even if I were so inclined, it would be futile to wish away a force that has moulded hundreds of generations, that governs some countries, and is a governing force in others, and whose absolutism has crossed national frontiers to sentence a writer to death for blasphemy. There is no safe distance from such a force, any more than there is from modern weaponry. Literature can hardly ignore this unfinished question.

I used to try to integrate my overpowering heritage, feel relaxed and easy about it, but I've discovered I'm not supposed to feel integrated and relaxed. It is not only inevitable, it is also perfectly natural for the inheritor of one of the earth's oldest and most complex inheritances to feel fragmented. And I have learned to treat my own particular muddle as a priceless asset. It is for my Third Eye to reconcile these fragments through fiction, and through my sense of a plural self to produce a fiction other than that which a less ancient, more homogeneous, more settled society produces. Time itself—an important event of the novel—is not the same in the Indian, especially the Hindu reckoning as in other societies, including other ancient societies that have suffered uprooting shocks and made clean breaks with the past. The city I grew up in had co-existing time zones. The past is so much with us, in the beliefs and routines people live by, in conversations whose allusions can go from legend to modern in minutes, that no time is ever entirely past. It is modern times that strain my own imagination, and I don't think anyone has succeeded in creating a modern Indian character, if by "modern" we mean a basic alteration or transformation from what went before. I'm not sure such a creature exists, so real life cannot be much help in providing examples. Is "modern" the frame of mind that descends from the European Enlightenment? Is it the position you occupy in the race for European technology? Is the contemporary western world still The World, and all other peoples to be judged by its yardsticks of progress? I've made some play with the word "modern" in my last novel *Mistaken Identity*.

One of the effects of coming to terms with my own dividedness has been to ignore chronology and to free myself from Indian locale and characters in my fiction. This has been liberating for me, and I expect it must be so for schizophrenic fiction in general. Not only is it time for interpretation to flow many ways instead of only west to east, but the question of direction is itself no longer relevant when the migration of cultures is leaving cultures open-ended, and when migration can take place without ever leaving one's soil. Where does one culture begin and another end when they are housed in the same person? There are powerful winds blowing through English literature. English is being assaulted by cross-currents of racial experience, by a vast expansion of its frame of reference, by new uses of imagination and language. The day of pure literatures, like pure or ruling races, is over, and English, at least, is in a new flowering—one that expresses a vision, a vitality, an expansionism that Sir Francis Drake and other English gentlemen never dreamed they would be unleashing when they set sail on their swashbuckling adventures.

To end with let me give you an example of the schizophrenia I am talking about. My father, a Sanskrit scholar, a fairly arrogant Indian, and a dedicated freedom fighter who was to die of British imprisonment a few years later, wept when London was bombed in the blitz, and when Paris fell to Hitler's armies. His answer to the question "Who am I?" would have been, "I am a member of the human race—and all the rest is rhetoric."

Political Commentary 1969-74

The End of an Era*

Recent events here in Delhi have been profoundly disturbing. In the decisions the Prime Minister has taken during the past month, and in the manner of their taking, this country has been driven to a crucial turn, a frightening turn. The three essential ingredients of our constitution are freedom, welfare, and social justice. In the supposed (and on analysis, doubtful) pursuit of welfare and social justice, we have taken a turn, perhaps irrevocably, away from freedom. There is an atmosphere of violence in the air—violence in the manner of the Finance Minister's dismissal, violence in the issue of an ordinance two days before the opening of Parliament, and violence in the tone of the Prime Minister's pronouncements at her mass rallies.

There is a sense of tragedy, too, that a great party, associated with great ideals in the past, has fallen apart and is in unseemly disarray. The cracks and fissures were there, but wise leadership could have held them together and enjoined unity in the interests of the Indian people, who have a long hard road ahead. In the past month the Nehru era and all that it represented in grace, in tolerance and above all, in its power to contain and sustain contradictions, has come to an end. We stand on strange, uncertain ground.

Any democratically elected government in India is always going to be accused of going too slow. Whatever measures it takes will never be far enough or fast enough to satisfy public opinion. This is inevitable in a country where normal economic development was arrested for some two hundred years during the British connection, where much remains to be done, and where, as a result, inequalities arouse disproportionate envy and disorder. This situation of need and lack is not a temporary one. It is going to be the condition for a long time. It therefore requires the most careful, long-term handling. Nothing can be more detrimental to it, and to the people's true welfare, than the stirring up of largely uninformed public sentiment—uninformed through no fault of its own, but because of our history—by catchy slogans that have little substance.

* *The Sunday Standard*, August 17, 1969.

The nationalization of banks appears to be such a slogan.

It has nothing new to add to existing measures. On all available scientific assessment it is even likely to end as a retrograde step, setting the economy back. If its purpose was to provide credit for the small-scale entrepreneur, this had already been introduced under social control. The banks have been cooperating wholly and up to date the measure has worked successfully. What needed to be done had already been begun, albeit without fanfare and without shaking confidence. The matter of rural credit, as seen by the experience of the cooperative movement, has turned out to be much more complicated than anybody imagined, dependent very much on particular farm communities and the various reasons why loans are needed, at times constructive, and at other times wasteful, as for marriages and dowries. A person of Mr. H.V.R. Iengar's knowledge and experience in finance has pointed out the unwisdom of over-simplifying this issue and the dismal results that may follow, with no benefit to the farmer and nothing to show for loans made.

These then are not simple matters of removing money from one place to another, or of siding with the "poor" against the "rich." The economy of a nation is more complex than such naive statements would have us believe. Extreme care has to be exercised when adjustments are made in it. In any case, presumably the government is on the side of the country, and progress in our circumstances, and under the form of government we have chosen, demands the cooperation of "rich" and "poor" alike. Such language and such distinctions smack of rabble rousing. They bode ill for calm and balanced decisions. They can succeed only in rousing an ill wind of which the final casualty may well be the country's progress. In all this it is impossible to avoid the conclusion that bank nationalization has much more to do with politics than economics.

Where does the danger lie? There are two aspects to it. Let us begin with the governmental aspect. In India today the purpose of government cannot be just to keep itself in power, because too much that is fundamental in establishing a sound social and economic order is at stake. Its purpose must be to provide a mature lead which works for the ultimate good of the people, not today's catch phrase. In this country for years to come, the central objective of any responsible government, of whatever political complexion, has to be more and more production. Nothing can take precedence over this necessity. The sharing of goods has to be matched by systems that will induce greater production. The government must adopt measures that will lead to greater productivity, if it has the good of the people in mind. No measure put through because of a power crisis and a personality situation can be called a responsible one. There is evidence that this has been the background of, and the reason for, the dramatic push-through of bank nationalization. It is a great pity that government has taken this serious step for a reason that adds nothing to public welfare and in circumstances that lend no conviction to its own action.

Nationalization is not a new word for India. Nor is socialism. Definite steps have been taken in these directions since independence. Under the leadership of Jawaharlal Nehru several vital sections of the economy were brought under government review and regulation. Steel and coal were included in the public sector and were greatly expanded to supplement the private sector. They were thus put in their correct perspective as a base for all essential economic development. This emphasis was also extended to manufactured consumer goods, e.g., cars. India insisted that no industrialist could put cars on the Indian market except with a definite time-schedule programme that would ensure the production of component parts within the country. During this period, too, the Indian Oil Corporation came into being and we achieved freedom from the Western oil monopoly. The hydro-electric projects were set in motion. Life insurance was nationalized, but with great thoroughness, precision and care. In all these activities, while the *objective* was radical, even revolutionary, yet the *methods* adopted were almost conservative in calculation, planning and execution, and above all, in avoidance of waste production. Mistakes may have been made, but one thing was clear: in the past we took whatever step we did because it was ultimately productive.

Bank nationalization does not belong to this category of action. With this measure, for the first time since independence, the government has taken a step for reasons that on the most impartial analysis do not indicate the promise of efficiency, of more money for the small man, or of any degree of eventual benefit to the economy. An economy which (except for West Bengal, and to some extent Bihar), was beginning after the recession to turn a corner toward stability, has just had a spanner thrown in the works. We are told that the government is carrying out a policy promised fifteen or twenty years ago. In this changing world when fifteen or twenty years pass, conditions alter, and anyone carrying out a twenty-year-old economic promise without due regard for its consequences *today* had better go back and study the present situation before taking doubtful plunges. So much for the governmental action.

But there is more to all this than the particular issue of bank nationalization, and we come now to the second aspect of the danger. Where does this path, adopted we are told, in response to great popular demand, lead us? In a year or two, perhaps less, people will be used to bank nationalization. The demand then may well be for the nationalization of the press, which is already hinted at almost daily in statements in the papers, for a ceiling on property, and for more and more controls of every kind. Where will this cycle end? The taste for blood, and it is very far gone in West Bengal already, is not easily appeased. It will descend more and more to the personal. Caught in this vortex it is not difficult to assess where our precious civil liberties will lie in a few years' time.

It took Nehru seventeen years of labour against gigantic odds to build a foundation for democracy, to instil in every one of us the notion of our cherished individuality and to establish and nurture the legal and national institutions to safeguard it. Private freedoms, it may be argued, are a luxury that under-developed societies cannot afford. Nehru, a dedicated socialist, believed otherwise. Freedom of thought, of speech, of the written word—freedom unassailable and inviolable—enjoyed to the fullest by the most ardent opponents of his policies was the hallmark of the Nehru era. Today that whole atmosphere where even disagreement could flourish within the law is being rapidly destroyed, and with it the emotional health that India, almost alone in Asia, possessed.

Freedom of Press in Jeopardy*

That important words do not have the same meaning they once had is becoming clearer every day. What is alarming, they are at times invested with unrecognizable meanings. The most fundamental of these words is freedom.

In explaining the Government's proposal to "diffuse ownership" of newspapers with a circulation above 15,000 a spokesman has said that the Government is committed to the freedom of the press, but that perhaps the word freedom needs to be differently interpreted. Freedom of the press will, he said, become a reality when each newspaper reflects all the shades of opinion represented by its working journalists and other employees, besides its editors and present owners. In no democratic country is every newspaper compulsorily required to reflect all shades of opinion, so this is emphatically a departure from press freedom as any free country understands it. It is a newspaper's right, in fact, to represent any point of view it wishes, even if, as Mr. B.G. Verghese of the *Hindustan Times* put it, it stands "in a minority of one." The highest duty of a free press, he writes, "is not to follow the mob but to lead and educate it." If the new proposal is to be taken seriously this definition will no longer have any meaning. An entirely new meaning of press freedom will prevail. Let us see what it will consist of.

The Government proposal destroys the relationship between shareholding and management. Normally share capital is the crux of investment. It runs all the risks of an industry, therefore it is entitled to a proportionate say in the management. This principle should hold true whether the majority shareholders are the workers in the industry, the general public or the Government. It is a vital link in order that control and responsibility should go together and the management should be a fully responsible one. No such link is evident in the Government proposal which lays down that while the existing owners' shareholdings will be limited to five percent, and the remaining ninety-five percent offered to working journalists, other employees and the general public, each shareholder will exercise only half a vote for each share. So, assum-

* *The Sunday Standard*, 19 September 1971

ing that *all* the shares in a newspaper are held by the original owners, the employees and the public, they will altogether still exercise only fifty percent of the voting rights. The remaining fifty percent of the voting rights on the management will go to a Public Trustee appointed by the Government. And if the general public does not subscribe to a newspaper's shares the Government will presumably have an even stronger hold over the newspaper.

The Public Trustee, the spokesman suggested (though this is not in the proposals), would not be a permanent fixture. He would hold voting rights only during the period that the ownership pattern is being broad-based. But as this period may be of uncertain and prolonged duration, this is not a very reassuring suggestion. An independent policy will obviously cease to exist in these circumstances and the role of editor will become redundant. The newspaper itself will probably become a causalty in terms of quality and efficiency. And whatever else the press will reflect it will certainly not reflect any opinion critical of the Government. This is the new prescription for freedom for the freest press in Asia.

Dissent has by and large played a thoughtful and spirited role in India since independence and no leadership has considered it a stumbling block on the road to an egalitarian society. Dissent has flourished in exact opposition to violence and provided the safety valve in many a situation that might otherwise have taken a violent form. It has also given Indians in every walk of life a fearlessness and unguardedness about what they say—a priceless confidence that will rapidly be dissipated once surveillance becomes a way of life. Nor can intellectual servility, which we will soon amply demonstrate, ever answer the true needs of any society. In the end the original, independent, rebel mind will be needed—and needed or not it will assert itself and fight for outlets, for that is the inexorable course of human aspiration.

Coming from the Government of a democratic country, therefore, this press proposal is a frightening one. Some noted editors have called it confused thinking. Unhappily it is not confused. Confusion and misunderstanding can be cleared through discussion. This has all the hallmarks of clear calculation, of definite policy, and whatever limited discussion has so far taken place between Government and representatives of the newspaper industry, has been careful to exclude any who do not support the official point of view. What else can one assume but that the Government intends to establish control over the channels of free speech and expression? It will do so under the mantle of progressiveness, and on the pretext of giving greater powers to working journalists and newspaper employees—a theory that breaks down at once on examination of the voting rights contained in the proposals. The worker will get a seat on the management but his voice will scarcely be heard. And the management will bear the powerful imprint of Government authority and decisions. This is some more of the fanfare of socialism without its substance. It is hard to see what benefit, apart from appearances, will accrue to the worker. What is only too plain is that if this proposal goes into effect it will systematically shatter not the bogey of "monopoly," but the reality of one of the healthiest, most stable institutions of our society. Surely some honest way can be found to associate working journalists and other employees with the industry in a productive and meaningful partnership, without gross Government interference and without thus endangering the independence of this sensitive and vital institution. Another question one cannot help asking is why the "diffusion of ownership" cannot begin with some other industry, where it will not arouse the suspicion that Government is bent on tampering with civil liberties.

The general trend seems to be toward an erosion of freedom, and it is taking place in the name of the Directive Principles of the Constitution, though we are yet to be told in what manner the Directive Principles sanction the destruction of our civil liberties. The process has been made easier by the removal of the Fundamental Rights from the constitutional guarantee. It may continue in the shape of the Law Commission which will investigate ways and means to promote the Directive Principles. There are good reasons why under-developed nations in our time have altogether dispensed with civil liberties—as in China and earlier the Soviet Union—with the clear-sighted objective that Government must take on absolute power to plan the nation's life and compel it out of backwardness by whatever means it finds most efficient. There is some logic to this. It is a defined policy and there is no expectation of freedom within its limits. There is, however, a high expectation of freedom in India and its steady erosion can benefit neither the Government nor the people. It can only create a vacuum into which rough forces can move without much difficulty. No social order dies except by its own hand, and that is what is happening here without any clear idea of what will replace it. Whether we are in for a spell of dictatorship of the Right or of the Left—and the signs indicate that it will be the former followed in due course by the latter—the consequences for freedom will be much the same.

In either case it is the minority that will suffer most. Not any particular religious minority, which is how we conventionally understand the term, but the minority of belief. The sufferer will be the dissenter, the independent thinker, the man who does not obligingly fall in line.

He is the one who will hang in the new order for no crime greater than "the colour of his hair." In the words of A.E. Houseman:

> Oh who is that young sinner with the handcuffs on his wrists?
> And what has he been after that they groan and shake their fists?
> And wherefore is he wearing such a conscience stricken air?
> Oh, they're taking him to prison for the colour of his hair.

And all this in a country where the most famous Hindus prayer recited by millions, the *gayatri mantra,* is neither a plea for personal salvation nor paradise, but for the light of knowledge and understanding. With this kind of majestic scripture and belief functioning at the level of the masses, an Indian may be forgiven for passionately believing that India can still make her way in freedom if she is given the chance.

The Vanished Art of Government*

When the Congress took power in 1947, it had had no experience in government, except for a brief spell in seven provinces from 1937 39. Its leaders were, however, politically mature men. They had served a long apprenticeship in the national movement. In the context of Mahatma Gandhi's programme, this meant they had encountered the problems of the countryside and learned to deal with them in practical and compassionate ways. They had an abundance of idealism, without which no battle for freedom can be fought, and Gandhi's movement was perhaps unique in history for its concern with moral value. It was this background that enabled the leadership at independence to take in hand with confidence the overwhelming problems that threatened to engulf us. They were thus able to rehabilitate a huge refugee influx with speed and efficiency, to successfully operate countrywide food rationing and distribution, and to set in motion enterprises that made the 1950s years of building and fruition. Their confidence was strengthened by the fact that the ordinary citizen felt a sense of participation and involvement with his government. There were failures, too, and a great deal remained to be done. But a confident start was made. It was a time of determination, of the will to get the things done, as well as of aspiration—the feeling that the path chosen was correct and deserving of hard work and dedication.

If the early post-independence leadership was a hybrid mixture of British liberalism and Indian nationalism, it was a highly successful mixture. It could be understood, historically, for what it was. It found echoes in the Indian past and it was relevant to the Indian present. Within its framework national policies that made sense both to the orthodox and the modern could proceed. It was also able to provide the faith essential to a situation where enormous difficulties have to be faced. Without this emotional and spiritual ballast to put heart into the arduous enterprise of nation-building, our effort, based on consent, might have fallen by the wayside. That so much was accomplished, that

* *The Sunday Standard*, 6 October 1974

corporate endeavours were launched and produced results, that institutions took root and flourished, and that India, with no great power status, was held in respect, and was an influence in international councils, is a tribute to the men who governed us and the manner in which they did.

Too much power held too long is bad for any political party in a democracy. When the calibre of the leadership also deteriorates and it is no longer concerned with values and standards, the results are painful for the party and the country. The Congress is a devastating example. (Cracks and fissures set in, the smear of corruption began to taint it, but these were for a considerable time held in check and off-set by a leadership whose standards of political morality were high and methods irreproachable.) The (other) check needed could only have been provided by the Congress having to compete for the country's favour with another party. This healthy development never came about, although the 1967 election did nevertheless point to the damage the Congress had suffered in the eyes of the electorate. In 1969, with its rupture, Mrs. Gandhi broke with the undivided party and declared she would usher in a new era with a new clean Congress, But she broke at the same time with the stern moral principle Mahatma Gandhi had enjoined—the marriage of ends and means—and which had been an article of faith with Nehru. The politics of power took its place, and an anchor of discipline, restraint and honourable dealing was removed from our midst. The need to capture absolute power and then to hold it at any cost brought a ruinous trail of consequences in its wake. Five years later the condition of the Ruling Party—its bedraggled standards, its half-buried skeletons, its cancerous dissensions—make the worst shortcomings of the undivided Congress look like a picnic. Today it appears to hold on to its mandate by sheer power—the power of money, manipulation and vested interests. Its most unforgivable failure, as far as the public is concerned, is its failure to govern, not surprising since it does not seem to know what it stands for. The Congress-CPI mixture, unlike the Mahatma Gandhi-Liberalism mixture, has produced neither a clear philosophy nor a clear programme. It carries the vocabulary and the frills, but not the reality, of the genuine Left. Sweeping into power on the rich rhetoric and lavish language of class war, its record has predictably been one of froth and swagger—the destruction of symbols, not real thought-out change, nor even the continued routine management of the country. In fact, routine management—the simple continuation of established standards of performance and achievement—is what has suffered most. From services which the citizen had come to expect, e.g. telephones and banks, down to his protection against a rising instance of crime, the failure of routine is frighteningly evident.

Even the procedures and norms laid down by Parliament have not been obeyed. The practice of governing by ordinance has been too freely employed. And now the concept and function of Parliament has been further injured by the disallowing of parliamentary privilege in the matter of the licence scandal. The Government's extra powers to arrest and detain, ostensibly to round up smugglers and other anti-social elements, spread a much wider net. We do not know how many student satyagrahis lie behind bars and what their offenses have been. We do not know if it is safe to disagree with the Government at all. The extraordinary arrest of Mr. A.B. Vajpayee is a case in point. A less well-known personality might still have been behind bars and the public none the wiser. These are signposts to the vanished art of government. Those who cannot govern resort to terror. Whatever ideas the Ruling Party started out with in 1969, today it is beginning to show the claws and wield the weapons of fascism.

Those who fail to govern must also resort to theatre, for where there is no bread, circuses must suffice. The campaign to catch and punish hotel and restaurant owners whose establishments are found with sub-standard or spurious products, is a highlight of the current circus. Proper government would go to the source, establishing rigid standards of weighing and packaging, and severe penalties for manufacturers who infringe them, so that nothing dirty or dangerous would reach the consumer at all. This would make it possible to check at which point actual infringement or adulteration has taken place and to pin down the guilty party, whether it is the manufacturer, middleman or retailer. The present campaign does not protect the consumer for presumably adulterated goods reach the market, and he can only find out through trial, error and expense what to avoid buying.

The star act of the circus is the catch-the-smuggler campaign. Since smuggling is a crime, why can it not be dealt with through the normal channels of the law? Would it be unwise to producer a smuggler in court in view of the embarrassment his evidence might produce to people in high places? And when the public knows that no one in the power clique can be accused or even mentioned in unsavoury transactions, and that the Ruling Party's collection of funds has helped to make the "parallel economy" a monster in our midst, the smuggler campaign alone will not solve the problem. Catching smugglers is long overdue, and it is excellent theatre, but all such campaigns would have more credibility if we knew that the Government was equally intent on rooting out the corruption in its own party.

"The system," announced a visitor to me, "has failed." It seems to me that if you deal deliberate, well-aimed body blows to any structure over a period of time, it is bound to "fail." That the political system we started out with survives, though not in its original health and vigour, is certainly partly due to the confusion in the Ruling Party's thinking. Where even a food policy—the crying need of the moment—cannot be formulated, more abstract conceptions are bound to be shrouded in a complete fog. Does the Government believe in our political system? Does it want some other? These questions, like so many others, float around undefined and unanswered. And the wait for answers may soon be over. The stirrings and rumblings of both the violent and the non-violent are heard in the land—Indians all, who in ways wise and unwise, will act to make India mean something honourable again, whatever system is found to contain the meaning of that forgotten word.

The Sound and Fury*

Democracy is not the important thing in India," the lady told me, "The important thing is social justice. Don't you understand?" The lady was Swedish. She had lived in India two or three years, travelled and made friends. She was genuinely concerned with our problems.

It is surprising how a dichotomy has been created between democracy and social justice in the past couple of years so that now it forms a kind of monotonous refrain in people's arguments, like an advertisement heard once too often and stuck remorselessly in one's head whether one believes it or not. Surprising too how some people in the West, who have thankfully discarded a lot of outmoded ideas and institutions from joint family to certain political beliefs themselves, continue to find these quaintly charming and even necessary in other cultures. Safe in their own free societies they are convinced that only some form of authoritarianism will push undeveloped countries into a better life. Hence the appeal of dictatorships for people who would never remotely tolerate a dictator on their own soil, and lately the glamour and publicity given to China's methods, parades and results. India has no publicity-mongers abroad, perhaps because we ourselves do not appreciate the immensity of what we have achieved.

I understood the lady all right. But what she did not understand was the fact that India, almost alone in Asia, had made a heroic attempt to combine the two, to bring a working democracy as well as social and economic change to the level of the masses, and that it had succeeded to a remarkable degree. The net result has predictably been dissatisfaction. Things have worked, but not fast enough, not efficiently enough. The atmosphere may well be ripe for reappraisal, for reform toward more speed and efficiency. But is it ripe for the demolition of a whole structure in the name of social and economic change, for a divorce between democracy and socialism—for the air is full of reckless manoeuvres to divorce the two.

---

* *The Sunday Standard*, 31 October 1971

There is no such explicit demand, of course. On the contrary, the voices of destruction keep pledging themselves to democracy with every axe blow they aim at democratic institutions. In the name of the people the fundamental rights were removed from the constitutional guarantee. In the name of egalitarianism the 25th amendment to the constitution now hangs like a sword held over common freedoms we have so far blissfully taken for granted of speech, association, work. The proposed draft scheme to "diffuse ownership" of the press is another supposed step toward democracy. The fact of the matter is that these are well-aimed blows directed at the destruction of an existing democratic structure and existing democratic institutions. And when all the damage is done, the freedoms provided by the constitution dismembered, the press reduced to impotence, the sound and the fury dissipated, what benefit will have accrued to the waiting masses? Who will be better fed, sheltered, educated at the end of it? How many more will be employed? Those questions will remain. And the failure to answer them, once attributed to the reactionary Old Guard in the Congress, next to reactionary elements in other parties and vested interests in the population, and at the AICC session in Simla firmly plastered onto the bureaucracy, will no doubt be heaped on some other convenient scapegoat. The fantastic statements made at the Simla AICC, that a mixed economy can be dispensed with, that the "monopolists" are the culprits responsible for all that is wrong with the economy, are not exactly indications of thought or analysis. And instead of being dismissed as nonsense these outpourings are not even challenged. They, along with other absurd statements, seem to acquire respectability with sheer repetition and the passage of time.

In vain one looks for some evidence of the working of a *mind* in all this—either collective or individual—for the assurance that these declarations and policies are the result of *somebody's* thinking. It may not be in agreement with one's own, but at least let us be assured that someone has given careful thought to a problem with the object of finding a practical solution. But only dramatic gestures and talk emerge. We are left with the strong feeling that we are living in an unintelligent time, led by people for whom power does not seem to be a means to an end, but an end in itself. Like all belief in power, this one is based solely on what is manifest in the here and now. It completely overlooks human potentialities and human growth. It completely lacks faith and true faith is rational. In India, for instance, it is quite rational to believe, based on our own past experience, that we can build a good social order governed by the principles of equality, decency and justice. That it has not been fully realized yet is no reason to destroy the instruments at our command.

The notion that destruction must precede a new order (Mussolini gave it the flamboyant title of "living dangerously") is far from sound. In its extreme form it shows an abnormal psychology, whether in individuals or in nations, a willingness to throw away what one has, what one has built through slow endeavour—not because it is rotten, but because one is incapable of loving and valuing it. Destruction makes a blaze and fireworks are attention-getting. But they are not a solution. Can worthwhile things not be built without this tragic waste?

Looking for some evidence of mind in our present national scene, one even begins to wonder what role "ideology" plays in all this—or whether tomorrow, if the public tires of extremes and turns more toward the Centre, the excesses will quickly die away and the leaders move adroitly toward the Centre. And with this kind of doubt about motives, there is really nothing solid for one to pin one's support on. I have no doubt that most people would do anything demanded of them. They would march enthusiastically with the Left, or make good cautious progress with the Centre, or go along with more Rightist policies, giving more scope to the private sector—they would in fact recognize and muster equal enthusiasm for almost any course of action, whatever its name or colour, provided it were practical and genuine. But so far they have been given no sign of either practicality or genuineness and in this drift the way lies open to violence.

Take Russia, take China, the Swedish lady told me, and she proceeded to draw parallels between these two countries and India, and to point out how India could benefit by their example. True, up to a point. Obviously there is a lot to learn from the rest of the world. But there is no real parallel between India, Russia and China. Our situations are historically, spiritually, fundamentally different. So there is no need to blindly follow their example. Russia at the time of the revolution was a land not of peasants, but of serfs. Russia with its vast open frontiers, its historic insecurity, its ancient acceptance of harsh extremes has, psychologically and environmentally, very different needs and values from India. China had been through twenty years of torturing civil war followed by Japanese bombardment and was on the verge of disintegration when Mao came to power. India is not cast in either image and there is a world of difference between these countries and India's character, her culture, her past and her present. There was never a better age than the one we live in for a country to confidently be itself and yet receive the help it needs for development from outside. At the root cause of our malaise may be that the leadership cannot decide what its objectives and priorities are.

In the midst of blasting the rich come such anomalies as a $ 37,000

Mercedes for the President's guests, and the tantrums of Members of Parliament who can only travel First Class on Air India. In the midst of the terror and tragedy of nine million extra people on our hands—with no sign of their dispersal in the near future—comes the announcement that the President will go to Iran at the invitation of a ruler who has announced himself in an interview to the French press as Yahya Khan's blood brother and stated his categorical support for Pakistan. Is it any wonder that we become cynical? The people of this country may well begin to feel with Bertrand Russell that "all politics are inspired by the grinning devil, teaching the energetic and quick-witted to torture submissive populations for the profit of pocket or power or theory."

Revolution and Counter-Revolution*

Revolution and counter-revolution are words much bandied about these days. The latest use we have of them is by the CPI in whose colorful language a "defeat rightist plot day" was declared for November 2 to meet the "counter-revolutionary" challenge of Jayaprakash's movement. We may therefore assume by deduction that but for Jayaprakash's obstructionism, revolution would be proceeding apace in India. This is certainly an interesting proposition for any student of political theory, or just an observer of plain facts, to examine. Revolution might well be proceeding apace and the majority of us may simply have failed to notice it. But let us recall the past in this connection.

Starting with Mahatma Gandhi's leadership of the national movement (which the CPI did not join) we had a kind of revolution. It was not revolution according to the Book, but it was a people's movement, cutting across class barriers. It wrought, in its way, fundamental change, for it brought the average Indian into the political reckoning for the first time in history. Gandhi's mud hut and his loin cloth did more to shape the political consciousness and the humanitarian goals of his era than blood in the streets or the barrels of many guns.

I believe that the post-independence years throughout the 1950s were revolutionary both in conception and achievement. It was a revolutionary idea that a poor, over-populated, underdeveloped country of Asia should embark on development within a democratic framework of government. It was moreover an idea that worked so efficiently under a mature leadership that the most cynical foreign observer, whether he looked into the working of our elections or our laboratories or even our gutters, had to admit after a few years that here was a healthy going concern. It was not going to be upset by outward threat or civil strife. Its institutions had taken root and its processes were orderly, a fact confirmed by the orderly succession after Nehru's death. As to Nehru's emphasis on industrial growth, I cannot agree with its critics that it was

---

* *The Sunday Standard*, November 1974

a mistake. It was natural, within the knowledge and experience of his generation, for modern men with a profound desire to dislodge this country from its backwardness, to opt for industrialization and science. Nor was agriculture bypassed. Agricultural universities were founded that played a crucial role in the application of science to the farmer's needs. Major irrigation and hydro-electric schemes were begun, and many completed, prior to 1964. It was for the successor governments of the 1960s to correct this emphasis where, whether it was due to inefficient working or policy itself, it had become productive or disappointing in its results, or to chart a new path altogether according to the lessons learned from the past. Lal Bahadur Shastri's government had just begun to make adjustments, to direct attention to small and medium industry, focus on particular problems of agriculture, and on near neighbours instead of a world role, when he died.

By 1966 economists the world over had begun to question the validity of growth, till then a cardinal principle. Affluent countries were beginning to be concerned with its effect on cities, on environment, on the disparities it created. And we in turn could look back with perspective on our own development and figure out which policies, well-reasoned in their time, had not paid dividends; particularly, how land reform, always a principal platform of the Congress, even before independence, could be speedily implemented.

Mrs. Gandhi, taking control of her party after its breakup, decided to take brisk action toward change, and nobody doubted that this was a society in need of change. But there was a contradiction inherent in her plans from the start. It was basic and it has still not been resolved. It was this: How can Communist theory and method be successfully applied to a constitutional parliamentary system of government, and in conditions where the press and civic freedoms give people a critical voice in affairs? The answer is that they cannot, and that without clear definition regarding both policy and value, confusion must result. In our case the existing system has been eroded, even deliberately damaged, without anything of working value taking its place. Vital amendments to the constitution have placed the fundamental rights in a grey legal area, while other institutions associated with a free society have been placed under continuous attack. While the leadership has thus played at revolution, no ghost of reform, not a flicker of real change has taken place. How could it? The CPI, Government's ally, has been during its entire existence, in the wilderness, often at bitter odds with the will and urge of the Indian people. Its generous quota of dedicated and educated men form an elite of prime theoreticians with hardly a practical notion between them, unlike their Soviet counterparts. The brotherhood of man is a noble idea, but to translate it into reality in Indian terms it took a Gandhi and a Nehru, both of whom functioned very well without the CPI's assistance. Mrs. Gandhi, caught in an unfructuous alliance of her own making, has found herself swinging now this way now that; now taking a measure, now retracting it, so that the government gives the impression of not knowing its own mind and fumbling along in an ad hoc way. Routine government has been replaced more and more by extraordinary authoritarian measures—ordinances, DIR, MISA—and in Bihar by a total paralysis of government altogether. It is as if a great country has been bound hand and foot and gagged, and lies waiting for deliverance—not for any magic remedies, but merely to be unbound and allowed to start working and living in an ordinary fashion again.

In this strange situation, standards of honesty and security have fallen, for the Indian public takes its cue from the top. If X of the ruling party can keep unexplained lakhs in his safe, or Y carry bundles of banknotes in his briefcase to bribe voters, and talk openly and vulgarly about it, so can a crooked businessman pull a trick or two without fear of penalty. So can the baniya charge double for rice and mix rubbish with his dal. So can the enterprising lawbreaker hold up citizens in broad daylight and beat them up before be relieves them of their wallets. Far from revolution, the current scene—where it has not ground to a halt in proper functioning—reveals itself in all the pitiful maladies that have grown and fed on dishonesty, inefficiency and lack of defined aim. A new set of politicians have become bosses of the countryside, with vested interests difficult to dislodge, since the wherewithal to dislodge them—through free and fair elections—can no longer be relied on. Those with Government blessing are apparently there to stay. Not even a Supreme Court order declaring an election null and void can displace them. And so we come to the need for change. For here are conditions intolerable to self-respect, an evil mess that decent men and women can no longer stomach—and this alone, more than hunger, more than hardship, can bring about change. Revolution in India has had its own distinctive face and run its own course. Mahatma Gandhi was nobody's idea of an avenging fury. Nor is Jayaprakash. Yet both represent revolution—the pitting of body and soul against injustice, the determination to fight wrongs. It is a great pity that the Congress and the CPI, singly and together, can only think of rallies and battalions to counter this growing stir. Mr. Dev Kant Barooah has lost no time in issuing a statement to all Pradesh Congress committees and State legislature parties, which for its element of fantasy rivals even his predecessor's string of amazing utterances. Directing State units to work with the CPI against Jayaprakash, he says: "In this task we should be ready to work together with . . . parties who share a common commitment to defence of democracy and parliamentary institutions." It is interesting to discover that the CPI is ready to defend parliamentary institutions.

Mrs. Gandhi's fear that Jayaprakash's movement is trying to remove her is surely somewhat irrelevant to the vital issues the movement is involved with. In democratic countries the world over, leaders are removed and replaced every other day, depending on their performance and popularity. Leadership is not a matter of divine right. The confusion on this as so many other issues, along with the autocratic concept of leadership the Congress has developed, stems from its partnership with the CPI. It is lése-majèstic now to criticize leadership and to replace it within the party is practically impossible. Long before the present regime started its drive against the country's democratic institutions, it had cut to size the criticism in its own ranks. But criticism rears its head nevertheless as we see from Congress affairs in several states and the need for revolution no longer waits for Congress to tidy its affairs.

Writings Connected with the Emergency
1975-77

Indira Gandhi's Emergence and Style*

I feel especially privileged to be here among you. I am not a historian, nor do I belong to any academic discipline, and I am definitely at a disadvantage in the presence of this impressive array of scholarship. I cannot, therefore, contribute to the battle of disciplines referred to by Dr. Gordon Johnson. I can only put before you, as a writer and a student of human nature, my reading of a present-day leader, and leave it to you to categorize and assess this leadership according to your own studies and findings in this area.

My paper will, I hope, throw some light on a most interesting and complex personality—as personality usually is—but in this case one who, I believe, is the key to the political atmosphere and events in India of the last few years—specifically those leading up to the Congress split in 1969 and thereafter; one who represents a dramatic departure from our past leadership, and indeed leadership as it has been discussed at this conference.

I have put down the sequence of events factually as they occurred, so a good bit of the paper is necessarily a blow-by-blow account. The only section of the paper that involves some personal knowledge, i.e., knowledge not drawn from my observation of public events, is the section entitled The Person. I hesitated to include this at first, but I did include it because I felt it may help to illuminate certain facets of the personality under discussion. Even without this section, however, there is considerable evidence of the independence and determination Mrs. Gandhi displayed before she erupted into the open in her new embattled incarnation, as it were. One of the most fascinating aspects of this whole study, to me, was that a personality whose clear outlines, if not its total image, were manifest in her statements and actions much before she made her bid for absolute power in her Party, could be so mistakenly assessed as merely quiet and correct, or docile, as the senior leadership most certainly did assess her in its extraordinary lack of perception—and to its own shock and dismay and somewhat comical

* Presentation at School of Oriental and African Studies, University of London, March 1974, introducing a paper on Indira Gandhi at a Conference titled "Leadership in South Asia"

consternation later.

The only assumption in the paper is my value judgement, implicit in what I have written, that freedom is necessary for the human condition, and that it is best realized within the democratic political system we chose at independence.

I'd like to direct your attention to some points in the paper. I have said that Mrs. Gandhi's bid for unfettered power within her Party had all the hallmarks of a coup. It also resembled, as I watched it, and some of the events that followed it, a performance, beginning with the dramatic, even sensational manner of the nationalization of 14 banks, and the initial street celebration arranged for it. There were at times elements of consummate artistry about that performance, such as I have referred to on page 23, where I speak of the double image Mrs. Gandhi presented with apparent ease and no sign of strain—being now radical, now moderate, and in each guise convincing and acceptable. There *was* a period of grim reality during the performance, when in fact the performance (or the feeling one had that it was one), had to be discarded entirely—during the crisis preceding events in Bangladesh and the war. I think that here, because reality was faced, and faced without froth and frills, she achieved great heights, both in successful strategy as well as in wisdom—It was wisdom to declare a halt to the war unilaterally, in a broadcast where her tone was restrained and statesmanlike, unlike her speeches earlier on the domestic scene. It may well be true of people generally, not only of politicians, that only coming to grips with a reality brings out the best and most courageous in them.

So, this bid for personal power, launched on what I would like to call "the people will not wait" theory—and certainly bids for power have been made for a variety of reasons, why not this one?—had these various dramatic elements. She was not unusual or original in thus using the people. Any historian or political scientist knows that the people have served, patiently and unasked, as the raw material of power. It is the politician, the "outsider," as Mrs. Rothermund put it in her paper on trade unions, and as Ram Chandra was in Dr. Panigrahi's paper, the one with greater education and opportunity, who articulates their demands. *How* he articulates them is a matter of his own beliefs and limitations and personality. *What* he draws from them is in part the reflection of what he himself is. What we see happening today in India could well be partly understood in the context of the leader.

We are a people who worship idols, so perhaps Mrs. Gandhi's theatrical instinct and showmanship were correct, and necessary. Perhaps something of a circus or a carnival atmosphere is needed to bestir us and catch our imagination. We are also a people nostalgic for great leadership, respecters of the family tradition, and she has, again perhaps correctly, traded on that. We are a people more willing than most to follow a leader. But we are also a people who yearn more than most for a good and great example to follow and have in the past even considered it a privilege to suffer, if the great example was before us. For that, more is needed than showmanship. Some substance is needed, and that is yet to come.

I have throughout asked myself the question I pose on page 19, of what Mrs. Gandhi intends, what, in fact, she is. I still ask it, and I know it has no simple answer. Perhaps today she herself cannot answer it simply.

In this background I would like to make a few general remarks in connection with my paper. An observation that Dr. Gordon Johnson made two days ago appealed to me greatly. He said something to the effect that change is not a value in itself, that part of the job of leadership may be to preserve what is valuable in a society; to see that change does not destroy what is well worth keeping. I believe that Nehru, and Lal Bahadur Shastri during his brief term as Prime Minister, understood this proposition—that change must take place, but that it must take place within the constitutional democratic order, as well as the federal structure, that India had chosen, both as a system of government and as an article of faith. I must emphasize faith, because in conditions where there is much to be done, and enormous difficulties in the way, clear values and a vision of the future beyond present difficulties are almost indispensable to daily progress, to providing daily sustenance emotionally and spiritually, to putting heart into the enterprise—without which no human effort, and certainly no voluntary effort, can take place. The choice of our political system was based partly on past history, i.e. the British connection with its liberal constitutional tradition. But, also, it was based on the belief that a country as large and as diverse as India could most *humanely* preserve its unity as well as its legitimate diversity within this system.

If it is argued that democracy is of no use in a developing society, that some more coercive system is a necessity, then I have no thesis as far as this paper is concerned, but I am one of those who believes that it does, and that India has been a heroic example of democracy at work, its institutions taking root over the years.

On the question of change, so vital in the study of a society, I venture to say that there has been monumental change in India since independence. The leadership after independence took defined and definite steps toward a socialist order which I will not list here. Some of these are listed in the paper. Therefore I do not agree with the argument in

Mr. Narasimha Rao's paper that socialism had no real content before the Congress split, that between Mahatma Gandhi and Mrs. Gandhi nothing much of importance happened. I would like to say exactly the opposite, that in fact nothing *less* than a revolution took place in India under Nehru. But revolution, like life, is a continuous process. It has to be continuously assessed as to its needs and priorities. Any leader can only do the best he knows, according to the needs and knowledge of his times. Some aspects of that revolution succeeded. Others failed. Nevertheless, in any assessment of those years, what stands out is that the Indian people were led, *within the framework of consent*—and that in itself was a gigantic experiment requiring a gigantic faith and effort—into a different dimension of life and expectation. You will, as political scientists, historians, economists and sociologists, find failures at levels and in aspects of this scene—as undoubtedly there were—but as Dr. Raychaudhri pointed out yesterday, a whole situation, a whole experiment, a whole aspiration has to be seen, not only its parts. And India's record in the 1950s was a record of success and failure, but above all, it was a record of remarkable aspiration. If leadership is to be judged by a competition for radicalism, then of course Nehru did not qualify as a leader. But it would be extremely useful if a scholar among you examined the Nehru era during the 1950s from the point of view of the kind and quality and quantum of change that took place in India. The evidence shows that constructive change, to whatever extent it took place, in the form of clearly defined and launched constructive programmes, any of them massive in conception, took place before 1967—which Mr. Narasimha Rao has correctly described as the watershed of the post-independence period. There has been no constructive change since then, allowing even for the disproportion of time and any extenuating circumstances. Mrs. Gandhi's preoccupation has been more with destroying the symbols of the old order than with the realities of a new order. There has been a visible and demonstrable decline and deterioration in every department of life, from the economy to all the standards, material and intangible, that we had built and attained—and certainly morale was never lower than it is today.

Every nation, every leader, every individual, to a certain extent bears the burden of his past legacy. But I do not believe that the present crisis in India can be substantially explained by the sins of omission and commission of the past, any more than a murder a man commits today can, beyond a point, be blamed on his grandmother and how she brought him up. Indeed it is difficult to understand—and perhaps one of you can explain it—how an unrivalled leader of national stature like Mrs. Gandhi, who attained absolute power in her Party in 1969, whose popularity was confirmed by the electorate in 1971, and rose to even greater heights in early 1972 after Bangladesh; who, during this process had succeeded in wiping out any opposition worth the name, and had an unparallelled opportunity, backed by immense goodwill, to put through her programmes for India, could have brought us to the state of crumbling disaster we are facing today, and in which the political system we live under, ultimately affecting the whole framework of our lives, is threatened. Is it unimaginable ineptitude, or deliberate destructiveness? Is it the wrath of God and nature, or the spectacle of a Party in disarray? I simply do not know. Or are we up against a combination of all these things concentrated in a personality who is quite simply determined to stay in power, whatever the cost?—aided without doubt by the fact that there is not at present the remotest coherent alternative. Perhaps you can supply the answer. I have been able to do no more than give you a picture and leave it to you to discard it if you wish, or assess it against the ideas some of you have yourselves formulated about leadership. Dr. Dalton has said that the requirements of a leader are 1) that he gain a sure intuitive understanding of his culture, allowing him to interpret its Great Tradition to his following, and 2) that this congruence places him in command of a viable method of political and social action. Dr. Aksari has suggested that the present ineffectiveness of leadership in India may be due to the fact that it does not proceed on the "inclusive" model, that it proceeds on a new model it has itself brought in. Dr. Johnson talked of a creative leader or politician, which I take it might mean the ability to assess the talents and possibilities of his people, as well as to be aware of the practical possibilities in a situation; what and how much should be attempted, and in what way. Dr. Brass has spoken of the inter-relation of power, principle and personal ambition. I might say that I am anxious to be proved wrong in my assessment.

In conclusion I would like to say that I have learned a great deal about my own country as I sat here listening, and I am indeed grateful for the invitation that brought me here.

10 Massey Hall
Jai Singh Road
New Delhi 110 001
May 14, 1976

Dr. R.S. Kelkar
Secretary
Sahitya Akademi
Rabindra Bhavan
New Delhi 110 001

Dear Dr. Kelkar,

Thankyou for your letter of April 20/21.

I wrote to you on August 27, 1975 on the matter of censorship, and you assured me in your reply of August 29th that you would place my letter before the President of the Akademi on September 8th. You now say that you have had no time to do so.

The question of free expression and the free circulation of ideas is crucial to a free society. I should have thought nothing could be as important as this to the Sahitya Akademi, which is concerned with writers and their work. Your failure to bring this issue to the notice of the President convinces me that the Sahitya Akademi of India does not concern itself with free expression. Indeed it seems willing to be a servile body, an obedient servant of dictatorship. Let me assure you that had Jawaharlal Nehru, its founder, been alive today, he would not have tolerated such a situation. Indeed he would probably have been in jail for he would not have kept quiet on any matter concerning human freedom.

I regret I cannot serve on any committee that is so lost to self-respect as to remain silent on the censorship that is strangulating India today. Kindly accept my resignation. I hope you will be good enough to convey the precise reason for it to the other members of the Advisory Board for English, and to place it on your records.

I am sending a copy of this letter to the President and the Vice-President of the Sahitya Akademi.

Yours sincerely,
Nayantara Sahgal

A Barbarous Situation

[Excerpts from Nayantara Sahgal's letters to the Authors' Guild of India, protesting against the censorship and suspension of civil liberties. She resigned membership of the Executive Commiittee of the Guild when the guild refused to put on record a protest against checks on freedom of expression.]

Since June 26, we have an "Emergency" in this country and the government has imposed censorship and suspended civil liberties. Tens of thousands have been imprisoned without trial. I consider this a barbarous situation. I personally cannot associate myself with any organization that seeks government patronage in these conditions much less be present at any function presided over by a member of this government. I would venture to suggest that there are issues at stake in India today that the members of the executive committee would do well to think about, particularly as to how they will concern writers in future, quite apart from how they will affect the entire country.

We are not faced with a "political" issue in a normal political situation. We are faced with a dictatorship which has ruthlessly demonstrated its policies and intentions. No further proof is needed of any government's utter immorality and shamelessness. I think myself, the country is more important than the Authors' Guild. It is in any case absolutely vital for all thinking, educated persons to declare themselves at such a time and not to fall meekly in line with the tyranny that now rules us.

The Emergency has made it clear, if any clarity were needed, what kind of government we are dealing with in its naked disregard of democratic functioning and human rights. I feel it would be totally lacking in self-respect to seek any assistance from it, much less make a patron of it. The western democracies you mention are democracies. They have not raped the decencies or destroyed hard-built institutions. There is simply no comparison between them and the present Government of India. I hope this situation will change but no change is brought about by a servile population and certainly not by an educated elite that falls in line with every excess a dictatorship commits. I am very certain that I can be no party to any of this.

The Clear Call of Conscience

The toughest thing in human history must be conscience. From Socrates, condemned to death for corrupting the youth of Athens with his ideas, and serenely choosing to die rather than "cease from my preoccupation with philosophy," to the stench of roasting human flesh and screams of human anguish that seem to arise from accounts of persecution in Europe during the cruel sixteenth century, and right up to modern times, there is very little doubt that whatever else can be stamped out and consigned to oblivion, conscience cannot. The evidence is overwhelming. Understanding the evidence is another matter. Why die of hemlock, or torture, or the executioner's axe, be burnt alive or torn limb from limb, if you can live? The answer is the mystery of mysteries, for what Socrates called the "search for truth" so cast its strange enchantment over men's minds that over the centuries even the terror of persecution faded and shrank in comparison. And it made no difference whether the search related to religious belief or scientific curiosity or opinion of another kind. Men stuck to it and paid the price.

The trial of Socrates is rather surprising, coming as it does during one of the most civilized eras in history. But it was an exception to the Athenian rule of tolerance and fortunately it came at the end of a long and brilliant career. Socrates had spent his days exposing the hypocrisies of his society. Every detail of his life and character were known to his fellow citizens. In his old age he was that grand and tremendous fact—a man who despising power and wealth and honours, and caring only for virtue, was ready to sacrifice his life for it. It was too late to prevent his influencing the whole course of human progress with his stubborn insistence that no one on earth had the right to tell another man what he should think or believe. Even his judges, all five hundred of them, were so impressed with his sincerity and integrity, that they wanted to set him free, provided he gave up his annoying habit of believing what he believed and teaching it to others. The trial does not record whether

* *The Sunday Standard*, October 26, 1975.

Socrates was amused by the idea of reprieving his life with such an impossible condition. But his courteous and implacable reply sounds as though he must have been: "If you propose to acquit me on condition that I abandon my search for truth, I will say: 'I thank you, O Athenians, but I will obey God . . . rather than you.'"

In obedience to God another man suffered the terrible death of crucifixion, and even in his agony forgave the misguided creatures who had nailed him to a cross.

These men were not intellectuals and they belonged to no elite. Socrates was a stonecutter's son and Jesus Christ a carpenter, members of what we today call the proletariat or "the masses." Yet what could be less like a mass instinct or urge than the agonizingly individual decisions they made, believing as the truly great have always done, that salvation is an individual matter. A man must square his account with his conscience, and life is not worthwhile unless he does.

The persecution of the early Christians actually had little to do with religious intolerance. It began because they insisted on defying the laws of the empire. The Roman police were willing to leave them alone as long as they kept their ideas to themselves. But of course they did not. They founded secret societies and went about spreading the gospel. If you are convinced you have good tidings of great joy to spread among the people, you are not likely to keep them to yourself. The men whose names live in Christian history as martyrs and saints embraced death with a kind of ecstasy. Hundreds of years later artists were painting inspired pictures of them. There they were, wounded with arrows, broken by stones, their eyes fixed on some vision beyond the pain. The apostle Peter even asked his tormentors to crucify him upside down so that he would have to endure more suffering than his Master. These we know about, the Who's Who, as it were, of martyrdom. But there were others, and the imagination boggles at their numbers, the endless stream of nobodies who went through every known torture and death; whose death provided an afternoon's thrilling blood sport for jaded appetites; and who need not have gone through any of it if only they had surrendered their belief. We don't know their names but we remember them as clearly as if each had been graven in stone or bronze for all eternity. Jesus was killed young, before he could organize a movement. It was these, his followers, who did the damage to the established order. And young as Jesus was when he died, it was too late to stop his message. The meek inheriting the earth, a loving merciful God, were ideas that caught fire like dry grass. Besides, he had died for them. Those who spread the word and suffered for it were men and women of the working class, sometimes slaves—until finally the message reached the throne.

Then, unfortunately, the throne and its ally, the Church, twin seats of power, became the persecutors in generations of slaughter of "heretics." Even reform in the Church made no difference to this cruelty because the reformers could be as savage in their demand for conformity as the parent organization they had defied and left. The reformer Calvin had a Spaniard, Servetus, burned at the stake because he did not believe in the Trinity.

"Heresy" was supposed to ruin souls, and heretics had to be killed to prevent them from contaminating other souls. But frequently heresy got mixed up with the existing political or economic setup and not religion, and soon authority began to spread its tentacles over all branches of knowledge and activity, because any one of them might be dangerous to souls. It became risky to say the earth moved round the sun, or that scientific experimentation was the only basis of certainty, or to talk about what you had come across in your researches in mathematics or astronomy or philosophy, or to make hilarious fun of the clergy responsible for the reign of terror. Yet oddly enough, people went on thinking and experimenting and talking and writing, though they were exiled, or their books burned, and sometimes the authors along with them. Obviously human curiosity is insatiable. If you have looked through a telescope once and discovered a star no one knew about, you are apt to go on looking, and discovering other things, and sharing your discoveries with others who are interested, because the task is so fascinating. If you have a book in your head, you are going to write it, even if it has to be written on matchboxes in the dead of night. These are compulsions even the Inquisition could not bully or control.

As early as 325 A.D. when the Christian Church became the official church of the Roman empire, the clergy were given the job of watching over books and banning the dangerous ones. That was all right when books took years to write by hand. But once printing was discovered, the job became a terrible headache. There were too many books to watch over. The clergy made an "Index" that became as famous as the Inquisition, listing all the books containing "forbidden knowledge" and warning writers of the consequences. Promptly the Index became a sort of best-seller list and a flourishing book smuggling trade between countries came into being, with book agents trying to get advance information about what was likely to go on the Index.

When punishments for non-conformity continued severe, some writers, Rabelais and Voltaire among them, had to move around rather nimbly, and sometimes take off for another country, to escape thrashings and other forms of displeasure when their sense of humour did not appeal to those they lampooned. But it did not stop them or others from writing. And their ideas—those irritating things that cannot be destroyed with their owners—gave birth to startling new worlds of dignity and beauty, of science and philosophy and government.

At about the time these worlds were being born in Europe, Aurangzeb sent for the nineteenth guru of the Sikhs and ordered him on pain of death to embrace Islam. Guru Tegh Bahadur refused and had his head cut off. But the story goes that he had told the Emperor he would perform a miracle by which his executioner would fail to do the dreadful deed. Writing a few words on a piece of paper he had tied it around his neck. When his head lay severed, the paper was discovered to read: "I gave my head but not my faith." Aurangzeb should have learned the lesson that only rebellion rises from the blood of a martyr. But history, it seems, is a very bad teacher. We never learn from it. The struggle between conscience and its killers goes on, and from some of the carnage brave new worlds come forth.

The India We Want to See*

It would be easier to begin by saying what I do not want to see, and that is India as a Power, in the accepted political-military sense, on the world scene. Apart from the destructiveness and immorality of the Balance of Power syndrome, I believe the quest for power has to be deliberately abandoned and consigned to the gutter by nations and individuals who call themselves civilized. There is no sign, of course, that this is happening. The quest is stronger than ever today, and as lusty among those who profess to follow Marx in the belief that national power and identity and loyalties must in time give way to a wider brotherhood, as among those who oppose it. Oddly enough the build-up of power is the bond that unites these two opposing ideologies. The nation state in all its array of military might, its spheres of influence, its wars and hard bargains driven for commerce, is an ugly crushing fact. And power itself is an overwhelming fact of life today, with governments, industries and individuals wielding far more of it than is good for them or others in most countries of the world. India should consciously reject power and power status as a goal.

Why should a nation in this day and age need nationalism? A true sense of selfhood does not depend on the inflated glorification of a nation, the trumpeting of its virtues, or the drumbeat repetition of what it stands for. What it stands for emerges clearly enough in the natural course if it is allowed to settle down into ordinary daily endeavour. And no drums and trumpets are needed to provide people with the basic amenities of life. If these are not there, there is nothing on earth to prevent a government from getting down to providing them if indeed it regards food, water and shelter as a priority. A nation that can produce weapons for war and put satellites into space can with much less expenditure cultivate its land and produce enough grain for its people. So I am assuming that in the India I want to see, I do not at least have to list food and water as desirable items. I am assuming that not too far in the future they will be there, for otherwise we do not deserve the inde-

* *Himmat*, January 23, 1976

pendence we won.

My own priority would then be education. National self-esteem flowers ultimately through the development of language, of industry, of science and art, and all of these have their starting point in education. Until it is widespread, related to our needs, and geared as much for adults as for children, there is no use talking about mature nationhood or the voice of the people. Uneducated, a man has no effective voice. He is the tool of other people, and the average Indian today is certainly the tool of other people. He is helpless, inert, a commodity to manipulate. He has to accept what he is told to do. Unhappily, many whom we call educated are in this category too, so it is clear beyond doubt that education is needed not only in the formal, or in any reformed institutional sense, but in a way even more fundamental. I have long felt that only Hinduism, thrown wide open to debate and discussion—for most Indians are Hindus—can cast some light on our character, can tell us why we are so rooted in timidity and submissiveness, and how we can be come men and women of decision and courage instead. Many lofty concepts arise out of education—equality, intellectual freedom, freedom itself. These are a long way from being meaningful until our people are educated.

When Mahatma Gandhi died, Nehru said: "The light has gone out of our lives." That light was created principally by example, by the tremendous fact of a man living what he taught. The India I want to see cries out for such a light, a living example among us to give us hope and heart for each day of difficult endeavour.

A Letter from Mrs. Gandhi's India*

On June 26, 1975, Indira Gandhi, using as an argument that the opposition had plans to overthrow the government, declared an emergency in India and arrested an estimated 1,00,000 citizens during the next few months. In later speeches she and other government spokesmen also insisted that the opposition was receiving money and help from abroad for its plans. She did not produce any evidence for her accusation, and no one accused of the monstrous charge of conspiracy has been produced in court to answer it.

According to the prime minister, the chief "conspirator" is Jayaprakash Narayan, for whom non-violence, in the tradition of Mahatma Gandhi, is an article of faith. Jayaprakash, aged 73, was released November 16, presumably because of his suddenly and dramatically deteriorating health in detention. Only the restoration of a free society in India will uncover the reason why he came so close to death in the hands of government doctors and in the care of India's two premier medical institutions, both government-owned, the All-India Medical Institute at Delhi and the Post-Graduate Medical Institute at Chandigarh. Now, cared for by private doctors in Bombay, he has made a partial recovery though the damage to his kidneys is permanent and he will never be normally active again. Another "conspirator" is Morarji Desai, also an apostle of non-violence. Aged 81, he is still in detention. Significantly, he has refused to eat any cooked food in jail, except what is, on occasion, provided by his family. These are perhaps the last two living Gandhian leaders of national stature now left in India. They did, it is true, wish most emphatically to replace Mrs. Gandhi's government, believing that in a democratic system governments are and should be replaced when they fail to fulfill their mandate or when they transgress the limits of decent and democratic functioning.

Mrs. Gandhi's government had clearly failed to fulfill the enthusiastic mandate it had received in 1971—a disappointment Indians could have lived with had her government not also come to represent

---

* *The New Republic*, 7 & 14 August, 1976

and shield growing corruption in its own ranks, and a vulgar and arrogant use of power that made a mockery of democratic procedures and the decencies of life. Her own insensitivity to the rising resentment against such behaviour and her refusal to consider specific charges brought in Parliament against ministers known to be corrupt, e.g. Bansi Lal (now defense minister) and L.N. Mishra (former railway minister, killed by a bomb explosion in early 1975) went far to aggravate conditions of severe economic distress. In 1974 a popular movement against her government took shape and a perennially divided opposition began to come together under Jayaprakash Narayan to discuss such issues as the erosion of citizens' rights, corruption that included the manner of collection and use of money by the Congress, and the need for electoral and educational reform—all of which had assumed grave national proportions. The demand that she should cleanse the Congress and take action against the corrupt began to be heard within her own party. It became obvious that there was a growing caucus within the Congress dissatisfied with her leadership, and who did not believe she had a divine right to rule.

When Mrs. Gandhi declared an emergency, she acted in character. Having become increasingly authoritarian over the past six years she finally took the plunge. Three events seem to have precipitated the decision. The election in Gujarat State in early June 1975 revealed that a united opposition could get the better of the Congress. With the general election due less than a year away, this was an ominous sign. On June 12th the Allahabad High Court judgement found her guilty of corruption on two counts in the conduct of her election to Parliament in 1971. The judge's courage caused a stir; his judgement did not. Her ambiguous and evasive statements in court, reported in detail in the newspapers, had left the public with the definite impression that she had been neither straightforward nor truthful. Her agent, Yashpal Kapoor, a highly controversial political figure, had made matters worse for her by his own brash statements in court. But above all, her own party seemed to be coming to the boil, alerting her to a possible move to replace her. Among those spearheading a dialogue with Jayaprakash Narayan and opposition parties, were the brilliant young radicals, Chandrashekhar, Mohan Dharia and Krishna Kant, who had in 1969 helped to engineer a split in the Congress, outwit the Old Guard and raise her to unrivaled leadership. Their brains, influence and backing could not be underestimated. After the Allahabad judgement, a group of congressmen openly urged her to step down pending the Supreme Court's decision on her appeal, in the interests of democratic functioning. When it became clear to her that she would not be allowed to appoint a substitute of her own choice to take her place, who would fade out in her favor later, she realized she was in real danger of not getting her position back.

The emergency paid immediate dividends. A sweep of arrests in the night had the advantage of surprise attack. Censorship immobilized the press. It also covered the country with an unnatural blanket of silence, for nobody knew what was going on. Criticism, oral or written, of the government, was forbidden. More than five people could not congregate without special permission. Permission was freely given to "spontaneous demonstrations" in support of the prime minister. And the flash and flourish of naked power left her party in no doubt about how far the leader was willing to go to keep herself in the saddle. Those still out of jail who had shown signs of rebellion had second thoughts. Armed guards were put on duty on the houses of cabinet ministers, ostensibly for their protection.

Once it was launched, the dictatorship was easy to perpetuate. The last few years had prepared the ground, providing her with a "committed" civil service which understood that it would not be tolerated unless obedience and loyalty to the prime minister were its first concerns; a police force built up to match the army in numbers, and in sophisticated weaponry and intelligence devices; a system of surveillance by which she kept her ministers and party members in line by the dossiers in her possession. Few of these instruments, except police control, were necessary in the countryside where the people were largely unlettered. But they were necessary in the cities.

Delegations of traders, teachers, students, workers, writers, businessmen and trade unionists were ordered to appear at her residence to congratulate her on the emergency and offer support to her "Twenty Point Program." Huge posters hailing her leadership, along with pictures of her in every shop window, burgeoned overnight. Anxious to overcome the charge in her own party and the general public of the Communist influence on her, she put a deliberate distance between herself and the Moscow-directed Communist party of India, her chief ally. She could afford to do so as she had Moscow's unqualified support. The CPI was obliged to go along with her, whatever its private thoughts about her new moves. These were headed by putting her much advertised "radicalism" into cold storage with concessions to industry, the withdrawal of a fixed bonus to workers her government had announced three years earlier, and a budget that cheered and mollified the rich. Her son, Sanjay, who had failed to produce an indigenous car for which he had been granted an exclusive government licence in 1970, generous support from industrial backers, and 290 acres of requisitioned land—and whose failure had become one of the now buried scandals of her regime—was projected as a "youth leader" and pragmatist, proof that the Congress was not committed to any particular ideology, only to progress. Sanjay was also projected as Mrs. Gandhi's political heir, setting the dynastic seal on her dictatorial coup, and setting at rest any speculation about who would succeed her. The Congress has thus been reduced to Mrs. Gandhi's personal possession to pass on, and India a classic example of Asian dictatorship.

In these circumstances, the question often put to her, of when she plans to lift the emergency, has become irrelevant, for lifting it will make little difference to India. Mrs. Gandhi has used her opportunity since June 26th last year to end all legitimate and constitutional challenge to her personal rule and to cripple the institutions through which that challenge could come. This has been done under constitutional cover. Parliament met from July 21 to August 7, 1975 to crucially amend the constitution and sanction—as the law of the land—the violations of civil liberties. Some 30 MPs were in jail—opposition leaders (except those of the CPI) and those belonging to her own party who she feared were going to lead a confrontation against her.

The censors in New Delhi and the state capitals whose job it is to black out news and opinions inconvenient to the government—and they cover the whole territory of newspapers, magazines, commentary, fiction, theatre and films—may be dispensed with once the emergency is lifted, but control of all media will continue. Radio and television are a government monopoly in any case, and in the past Mrs. Gandhi has used them blatantly to promote herself and her party and distort happenings in India. Now a single news agency, Samachar, feeds the press with official handouts. Respected editors have been thrown out of their jobs and replaced by sycophants, and newspaper management, already government-manipulated, will soon be its complete tool in what the minister for information and broadcasting picturesquely describes as "re-structuring the entire newspaper industry so as to make it accountable to the people." In today's official jargon this means government's iron hand. This week two of the last dissident voices were silenced. A one-man weekly, *Opinion*, was simply shut down; a tiny circulation monthly read mostly by intellectuals, *Seminar*, put itself out of business rather than submit its pages to the censors. The power of the censors is reflected in the fact that, as of this writing, not one of the supine Indian press has reported the untimely death of these periodicals.

A new law was passed last August making election disputes relating to the president, the vice president, prime minister and speaker nonjusticiable. And the Representation of Peoples Act was amended retrospectively in order to legalize the very issues on which the prime minister had been indicted in her election case—an extraordinarily brazen piece of legislation since her case was already pending in the Supreme Court. Thus any genuine judgement by the court was nullified in advance. With no legal scope left to operate in, it was obliged to exonerate her. The lesson of those who rebel foreclosed other options.

Even if the emergency is lifted opposition parties will take long to recover from the bludgeoning authoritarian rule has given them. Thousands of their political workers are in jail and a relentless campaign to discredit them as enemies of the people is carried on by the government in circumstances where they are not free to answer charges or be reported in the press. They would find themselves severely damaged in human resources and in funds if an election were announced, and without the full restoration of press freedom and civil liberties there can be no free and fair election. No one expects one either.

After the political opposition, Mrs. Gandhi's main target has been the universities. Delhi and Nehru universities, both in the capital, and among the country's most prestigious institutions, have been subjected to searches and arrests. At one time, soon after the emergency was proclaimed, nearly the whole Sanskrit department of Delhi university was in jail, a warning to those who had Jan Sangh (Right) affiliations or sympathies. But followers of the Communist party—Marxist, which is bitterly opposed to the regime, have not fared much better. People with a living to earn and families to feed will think twice before openly dissenting.

Lifting the emergency will leave intact the vast police force, as big as the army and inflated with powers. Law and order is a state subject but the Border Security Force, used for defense, is far better armed than the normal police force, and has been freely used along with the powerful Central Reserve Police against citizens. The government showed its police might and muscle when it arbitrarily dismissed Tamil Nad's opposition government on January 31st, instead of holding the state election due at the time, or postponing it for the duration of the emergency as the general election has been postponed.

Censorship has been the most highly effective instrument of India's dictatorship, keeping people ignorant about an event in another town or even half mile away in their own town. The enormity of censorship, we now know, can never be understood by people in countries where information is freely available, where there is a continuous flow of news, and where views of all kinds can be freely expressed. Indians today are in ignorance about what is happening in India and only those world events reach them that the censors pass as suitable for consumption. Very few people heard about the non-violent protest begun in Delhi and four states (U.P., Bihar, Maharashtra and Andhra Pradesh) on November 14th, Jawaharlal Nehru's birthday, and concluded on January 26th. Republic Day, though it daily offered up batches of peaceful protectors to the police and was led by citizens as eminent as Maniben Patel, Sardar Patel's daughter. Several jailbreaks, major news items in ordinary times, were not permitted to be reported at all. News about them traveled by grapevine. But one has learned to read between the lines of newspaper accounts. This does not take much ingenuity since our leaders have become drearily repetitive and the current jargon they use provides definite clues to their statements. Reference to "rightist fascist forces re-grouping" means the opposition is refusing to surrender or be wiped out. One positive result of the emergency, in fact, has been to bring a divided opposition closer together and to blur the barriers between left, right and center. As in British times, the issue is freedom. When senior officials meet in Delhi to discuss stricter security measures along with the transfer and dismissal of jail staff and officers the perceptive reader realizes the jailbreak accounts he has heard must be substantially true.

In April the family planning drive, an objective with which there is widespread agreement among the educated, made inadvertent news when bungling and bullying tactics misfired, leading to an angry demonstration at Turkman Gate, a predominantly Muslim locality in Old Delhi. This was not, of course reported in the newspapers, though the crowd turned violent, leading to a riot, with 30 or more people killed and hundreds arrested. But the news was too explosive to be contained and word of it spread fast. Earlier the Delhi administration had announced that anyone expecting a third child would not get a ration card; government-employed teachers would have to get five people sterilized if they wanted to keep their jobs; no one due a government house allotment would get it till he produced a sterilization certificate; and vans had rounded up young and old, married and unmarried for "the operation." The fury at Turkman Gate had been in response to forcible evictions of its inhabitants from the area along with the administration's family planning methods. That there must be some truth in the news of deaths and arrests on a considerable scale became evident when about a week after the event an array of spokesmen swung into identical explanation like an orchestra with everybody playing the violin. The lieutenant governor of Delhi denied that people were being forcibly sterilized. The health minister hastened to make it clear in Parliament that the union government "was not for pressure or harassment in implementing the program" and was ruling out compulsory sterilization for the parents of more than two children. A team of reporters sent to "investigate allegations of forcible sterilization" found them "entirely false." And a government release stated in predictable language that "certain unsocial and frustrated elements were circulating rumours that rations would not be issued nor salaries paid to persons not undergoing sterilization." It warned the people to be on guard against "such anti-national and anti-social elements and their nefarious designs." None of this vehement denial explained why the new family planning center set up with much fanfare at Dojana House, Old Delhi, had abruptly been shut down, nor the flood of resentment that continued to fill the air. But this unceremonious retreat on an issue where the Catholics had already expressed firm disapproval, and the Muslims had flared into actual violence, is an interesting aspect of manoeuver required even in a dictatorship. Modifying Delhi's rough sterilization drive is probably based on an assessment that the subject is inflammable and the Muslims must be handled with care. But in our irrational political situation it could simply be based on the possibility of a third expected child for Mrs. Gandhi's elder son. In any event it would be a tragedy if the campaign is not soon converted to education and effective remedy, for on this issue, emergency or no emergency, we cannot afford to fail.

The Romance and the Reality of Mrs. Gandhi's Rise to Power*

On June 26, 1975 when Indira Gandhi declared an emergency, imprisoned leading opponents and critics, imposed censorship and launched a police state, arresting some 100,000 citizens without charges or trial over the next few months, her behaviour was not entirely unexpected. Democratic modes and manners are not every politician's cup of tea, even within an established democratic system, and Mrs. Gandhi had demonstrated for several years past that they were not hers. The emergency halted two developments: a multi-party movement, the Janata Front, under the leadership of Jayaprakash Narayan, that was becoming a political challenge to the Congress party, and her party's move to choose another leader when a High Court invalidated her 1971 election to Parliament for two violations of the election law, requiring her to step down. She had travelled a stormy road since 1966, from formal decorous nomination by her party to the Prime Ministership, to a whirlwind break establishing her individual identity and following, and finally to the decline of her popularity. Between what Indian newspapers described as the "Indira wave" in 1971 and the "anti-Congress tornado" of its by-election defeats by the Janata Front in 1975, climaxed by its defeat in the Gujarat State election in June that year, lay the rise of individual authoritarian power and the backlash it inevitably creates in an open society. Mrs. Gandhi met the backlash by bringing the curtain down over the whole democratic process. The national election due in March was postponed for a year, and later postponed for another year. Recently Mrs. Gandhi announced the March 1977 election would he held after all, a sudden reversal characteristic of her dramatic political style.

Drama has been manifest both in her statements and her political behaviour. Recently she said her education had taken place "in the jails of India, the fields of India." She has often referred to her sacrifices for the freedom struggle, telling an interviewer in 1969 the British Govern-

* *The Times* (London), 11 March 1977

ment had regarded her as so "dangerous," it had not allowed her even the minimum prison facilities given to other political detainees. This view, with jail by implication a repeated experience, and an upbringing close to the Indian masses, is more romantic than accurate. Mrs. Gandhi went to jail once, for eight months, September 1942 to May 1943, during the last phase of the national movement known as the Quit India agitation. She had no part in the nationwide civil disobedience of the 1920s and 1930s. In the 1920s she was too young. In the 1930s she was a student in Switzerland and England, intermittently with her Indian schooling, learning French, travelling in Europe with her parents, ending up at Oxford, though she did not get a degree. She was nearly 25, and a bride of six months, when she went to jail in 1942. She was interned in the same barrack of Naini Central Jail in Allahabad as her aunt, Vijaya Lakshmi Pandit, her cousin, Chandralekha Pandit, and a number of friends. As prison experiences go, it was a reasonable one, according to the diary her aunt published of this period. Indira and her aunt, as members of the Nehru family, were shown special consideration by the British Government and the jail authorities. They were allowed books, letters, fruit and interviews with their husbands, who were in the men's section of the same jail. Indira who kept poor health was weighed regularly and a careful check was kept on her physical condition. Mrs. Pandit's diary of the time reveals that both Indira and Chandralekha showed guts and imagination in making light of the whole experience. Much later, as Prime Minister, Mrs. Gandhi told public meetings and Opposition party, the Jan Sangh, wanted to murder her. She had to withdraw the statement when angry Jan Sangh Members of Parliament demanded an explanation.

Mrs. Gandhi's descriptions of her childhood are bleak. The great and glowing experience the fight for freedom became for Jawaharlal Nehru and his wife, remained for her a dark and sombre one. Her games, she says, consisted of fiery speeches to her dolls, triumphant encounters with the police, and social work since the age of twelve. Yet few parents could have striven as hard as Indira's to light up living for a cherished only child. Tragedy touched her at 18 when her mother died, but opportunity and privilege helped to smooth the path ahead. Her career in politics was taken for granted. As Nehru's daughter she entered the Congress party at the top, not tnrough the rough school of competition. In the mid-1950s she became a member of its executive body; in 1959, its president; and seven years later, Prime Minister. Each step was smooth, aided and desired by the party's influential leaders. The Congress party had created a climate during the national movement of opportunity for women, and taken pride in their achievements.

The daughter of the dearly loved, charismatic leader, Nehru, was doubly blessed. No gentler, more supportive environment existed for the leadership of a woman. Hardly a citizen of India remained unmoved, with memories of the role her family had played, when she took the helm. It seemed apt and beautiful that a child who had belonged to the country's aspiration for freedom had come to its highest political office.

It had been natural for her as a child, in times calling for patriotism, to see herself as a beleaguered heroine, a Joan of Arc leading her people to battle against the foreigner. But the fancy did not end with childhood. As a politician Mrs. Gandhi seemed to see enemies in the legitimate opponents a democratic system of government throws up, conspiracies in open organised peaceful protest. It was an approach that fogged the rational political atmosphere inherited from the Nehru era with innuendo and implication. In 1969 the ruling clique in the Congress which had elevated her to the Prime Ministership, showed signs of wanting to replace her, an uncomfortable but fairly routine situation every leader in a parliamentary democracy faces. A vote in her party would have decided whether or not she had the majority to carry on. Mrs. Gandhi did not ask for it, perhaps because she was extremely doubtful of its outcome. Enlisting the support and techniques of the Communist Party, she took her campaign to the streets. Backed by emotional propaganda proclaiming her India's natural leader because of her Nehru birth—a strange anachronism for one who claimed to be modern and at war with all that was anachronistic in India—Mrs. Gandhi spoke of the "plot" against her in her party. A bitter and startling performance, it shattered the orderly disciplined procedures of Indian politics. This was "politics" too but of an unexpected kind. In a country where democratic institutions had been served scrupulously by two Prime Ministers since independence, and every effort made to inculcate a modern scientific approach to life and politics, Mrs. Gandhi's emotional appeal took the country back two hundred years to the idea of personal, dynastic rule.

But street arousal and the promise of a new world are exciting. Mrs. Gandhi said she wanted to cleanse the Congress, bring radical change to the country, and could only do so if she had effective command. The argument was appealing. In 1971 the electorate voted her to power at the head of a New Congress. The old party was now in the Opposition. By the end of 1972 the Congress rebels who had fought to put her in supreme command were disillusioned by her performance. A grain policy, launched with radical fanfare but with little preparation, had disastrously failed to provide grain. It had antagonized farmers, led to food riots, student demonstrations and bread queues, thoroughly discrediting

Government's effort to become a monopoly buyer of foodgrain. The New Congress alliance with elements of big business produced an atmosphere of moral decay when methods of fund-raising for the party laid her important colleagues open to corruption charges. And Mrs. Gandhi's establishment of a single line of command in the party, her control of the party machine, and her intolerance of politicians with a strong popular base, created the fear that she was on the road to authoritarian rule. This was borne out by the processes of centralization she set in motion, depriving State governments of initiative and relying heavily for her own sources of power outside normal political channels, on three paramilitary forces and the intelligence network. Between 1969 and 1975 the police budget doubled, and the Opposition—Left, Right and Center—faced a massive confrontation with the paramilitary forces under Mrs. Gandhi's control. By the end of 1971 the Communist Marxist Party (distinct from her ally, the Communist Party) had been weakened and battered by "police encounters." During 1974 the police were used to crush the railway strike and to confront the non-violent multi-party movement led by Jayaprakash Narayan. All this was made possible by a law passed in June 1971 giving the Government powers to arrest and detain without charges or trial for a 6-month period. Under the emergency, the period extends to two years.

Considering her family's prominence, surprisingly little was known about Indira Gandhi when she became Prime Minister, so little that each departure she made from conventional political behaviour during the next decade startled the public. At the personal level she was guarded, remote, inarticulate. She did not reflect the wide educational opportunities she had had. People knew her as the mother of two sons and, after independence, her father's hostess and companion in New Delhi. She had been widowed in 1960 and for much of their married life she and her husband had been informally separated. The family circle knew her as headstrong and determined, yet the Congress party chose her as Prime Minister in 1966 believing she was manageable, self-effacing and would listen to advice. She did not have her father's intellect, his capacity for long-lived friendships and affections, or the warm human qualities usually associated with charisma. These were considered points in her favour. The Congress was looking for a patient cooperative plodder in circumstances when the party needed to pull together.

No one gave a thought to her democratic credentials. Seventeen years under Nehru's leadership and nineteen months under his successor, Lal Bahadur Shastri, had accustomed Indians to free political institutions, the climate of dissent and debate. It was taken for granted that the leadership of India meant the service of these. But apart from this, Indira was Nehru's daughter, and Nehru had been a thoroughly known quantity. His political ideas, personal tastes, strengths and weaknesses were on record in his books and speeches, in all the facets of the crowded career he had lived in the public gaze before and after he became Prime Minister. One quality dominated the rest. Nehru had an abiding respect for other opinions. A national hero, with the adoring regard of his countrymen, he could at any stage of India's first tumultuous years of independent nationhood, have seized upon a valid or illusory reason to become a dictator. He chose to govern as a democrat, treating leadership as a trust to protect the people's growth in freedom until they were educated and experienced enough themselves to do so. It was in this context that the Congress party elevated, and the electorate accepted Mrs. Gandhi as a leader. It is this trust that those who have now broken away from her party believe she has betrayed.

The March election will be held under the emergency though press censorship has been suspended, and we are told political prisoners are being released and all activity connected with the election allowed. But Information Minister Shukla has warned that "the press will be expected to abide by the laws of the land." One of these laws, enacted under cover of the emergency, prohibits publication of whatever the Government considers "objectionable matter." In substance, criticism of Mrs. Gandhi or her Ministers now constitutes a penal offence. Under a recent constitutional amendment Government also has wide powers to suppress "anti-national" activity and organizations. With the changes in law since the emergency, the term "political prisoners" may not even apply to many thousands in jail, who may now be construed as criminals. The release of known political leaders is different from the release of the thousands of political workers a party relies on to prepare for an election campaign. And over and above these limitations Government continues armed with arbitrary powers of arrest. Freedom of expression and activity are thus now entirely at the mercy of the executive, and with the sweeping constitutional amendments passed last year, the executive is in effect the Prime Minister, unaccountable to legislature, judiciary or country.

The Opposition has nevertheless accepted the challenge. A section of it outlawed, the rest of it handicapped by the arrests, harassment and censorship of the past twenty months, its acceptance can only be construed as a valiant hope that even in these circumstances it is worth doing battle. Events have shown that the effort was indeed worth making. The processes halted on June 26, 1975 have sprung to immediate life. The Janata Front has attracted huge enthusiastic crowds as people have thronged to cheer Mrs. Gandhi's prisoners. The resignation from her Cabinet of Jagjivan Ram to form a new group, "Congress for Democracy," in alliance with Jayaprakash Narayan completes the split that was pending on the eve of the emergency. The issue has been reduced to freedom versus slavery, and there seems little doubt, if the elections are free and fair, which the masses will choose. The agony and disenchantment of those who fought for freedom is symbolized now, too, by the presence of Nehru's sister, Vijaya Lakshmi Pandit (Mrs. Gandhi's aunt), in the Opposition. Mrs. Pandit, who resigned her seat in Parliament in 1968, and retired from politics, has been careful until recently to make no judgements of her niece, though her disapproval of authoritarian trends in the country during the past few years was well known. Her return to politics is symbolic at this time of the widespread feeling that India must return to the values Jawaharlal Nehru stood for, and which the ruling party led by Mrs. Gandhi no longer represents.

Introduction to *A Voice for Freedom**

I had lived in Delhi nearly two years and written for newspapers on a variety of subjects when the Congress split in 1969 riveted my attention to the political scene. Something different had struck it with the impact of a blast. This was not a parting of the ways based on genuine differences of opinion and programme. This was an emotional bid for personal power. It made a carnival of principle, procedure and convention—dull words, of no use at all for street arousal—and went on to make a carnival of politics and economics.

By 1971 it was clear to me that Indians were being pushed toward an authoritarian order. The country would be slipped into it if possible, and bludgeoned into it if necessary. One significant sign of this was the condition of the Congress itself. It was being deprived of discussion and debate. Its rungs of command were being cut away. The good leadership material within it was being held in check, and later dispensed with, while obliging mediocrity was brought forward and put in key positions. A party that ignores its own constitution, and stifles its own democratic processes and available talent, is obviously not committed to or concerned with democracy in the country or a free society as a value. A ruling oligarchy was emerging, some of whose leading lights were transferees from the CPI.

No propaganda effort was spared to set up the one-party one-leader idea. Eventually the Emergency gave its seal and sanction to this development in a series of steps. Mrs. Gandhi had the law changed to immunize herself—a leader above the law—against the Allahabad High Court judgement. Congress President Barooah informed his party and the public that India was Indira and Indira was India—and no one contradicted him. A proposal was circulated, and later withdrawn and disowned by the Government, advocating a "presidential form" of government for India, headed by a president armed with considerable personal powers. And finally, in 1976, came the amendment package in Parliament that made the Prime Minister a virtual dictator. In a nation

* Published by Hind Pocket Books, 1977

reduced to silence, even dynastic succession could be unabashedly promoted. But these trends in the making were visible much earlier than the Emergency, and it needed no special insight, only an observation of events, personalities and atmosphere to recognize them.

To my surprise not many who should have, did. In Delhi the breed known as "intellectual" seemed happy to repeat the current "socio-economic" jargon and to believe we had entered an era of real change. Disagreement with those at the top was apt to earn one the label of "reactionary," and certainly the cold shoulder as far as recognition and opportunities went. I remember feeling a tremendous relief when in December 1973 Jayaprakash Narayan issued an alert in the form of a letter to Members of Parliament, and one to youth, urging ways and means of protecting our civic freedoms and democratic institutions, and setting up Citizens for Democracy for this purpose.

The Bihar Movement grew out of this and related needs the following year, and became a massive, organised, peaceful protest, first against the ineffective Bihar government, and later against the Union Government's refusal to listen to just demands. Its popularity and the success of its demonstrations, due in part to the co-operation of sections of the opposition, gave the opposition its first platform for national unity, and this had an immediate effect on its performance in Parliament and state assemblies, on by-elections, and finally in the Gujarat state election in June 1975. It confronted the Congress with the first serious political challenge it had faced since independence. Combined with the Congress party's own opportunity to replace Mrs Gandhi after the Allahabad High Court judgement, it resulted in Mrs. Gandhi declaring an Emergency.

As a political writer for the *Indian Express* I had been a critic of what I saw as the main current since 1969, a muddled "radicalism" masking the growth and entrenchment of personal rule, unaccountable, it seemed, to any forum. So I had been an outcast with the Establishment for several years before I became interested and involved in JP's experiment in Bihar and a columnist for his weekly, *Everyman's* in September 1974. By that time the Establishment looked upon me with grave suspicion, even as something of an aberration as a member of "the family" who did not seek patronage or make obeisance, and who refused to be squeezed into line.

It will illustrate the mood in the capital when I say that the more timid among my acquaintances in and outside official circles stopped coming to my house at this time. A friend of many years in the Foreign Service confessed it would be awkward for him to do so. A journalist doing extremely well under government patronage, who had once solicited my articles for her page, found herself unwell or otherwise occupied on the two occasions I invited her to meet friends at my apartment. I was, in fact, surrounded by signs of disapproval. A relation of mine remarked that on a trip to Bihar I had wandered around with *goondas*, not a very accurate description of two young activists of the Bihar Movement in whose company I had visited Arrah. The Supreme Court lawyer who accosted me (there is no other word for it), at a dinner party in Delhi to inform me I was "marching out of step," and told me to change the tone of my articles as well as the newspaper I regularly wrote for, is another example of the lack of mind or manners with which power so often infects those on the comfortable side of it. In Calcutta on a visit in early 1975, my sister said that Chief Minister Siddhartha Shankar Ray had told her with a mixture of seriousness and humour, in reference to my newspaper writings: "We could pick her up under MISA any day."

There were signs, too, that the ardour with which I had been wooed as a writer was fast fading. A lecturer in English at Delhi University, commissioned by the American publisher Twayne, to write a critique of my work, and who had taken material from me for his project about three years earlier, simply vanished from my acquaintance. A film maker, enthusiastic about filming my novel *This Time of Morning*, abandoned the idea after obtaining funds from abroad and deciding on the film stars who would play the leading roles. She said by way of apology that the book was too difficult to film and she hoped I would write something with fewer characters—though the characters in the book had not grown in number since she had read it. I came to the conclusion that the lecturer found it politic not to connect himself with me. And the film maker, who lived abroad at the time, probably discovered during her two-year wait for funds that I was too outspokenly opposed to the government to risk her own acceptability with the ruling clique. The areas of television, information and broadcasting—her special concerns—needed government's direct sanction for programmes.

Such indications, while they were profoundly disturbing as evidence of the narrow, rigid atmosphere about us, and the kind of either, or line-up it demanded, also served as excellent material for writing, and I put it to good use. Two novels, *The Day in Shadow* and *A Situation in New Delhi* reflected the mounting unease and at times the feeling of impending disaster I had as I wrote them.

The time served me well, too, because it put me in touch with men and women in the opposition. It seemed to me there was far more going on there both in idealism and practical thinking than in the now servile ranks of the Congress. Opposition talent came from the professions, the trade unions, the universities and the countryside, from the Right, Left and Centre. I was impressed by the spectacle in Bihar, of an organised, disciplined youth movement, committed to non-violence and change. Their meetings and activities were more stirring than anything I had seen in twenty-five years. The more I saw of all this, the more absurd and dangerous the Delhi delusion of a one-party one-leader system looked. Some obliging entrepreneur had by now put up a huge poster proclaiming this idea in Connaught Place. It gave me a shiver down my spine each time I passed it.

When the Emergency came, like a numbing blow in the dark, the manner of it was shocking though the word "dictatorship" was common usage by then. After Mujibur Rehman's establishment of a dictatorship in Bangladesh in early 1975, many in India waited for it as we wait for the monsoon, knowing that, sooner or later, it is coming. JP warned a public meeting of the possibility. But no one realized how soon or suddenly it would come, and how well-executed it would be. Suddenly we inhabited a police state. Unknown tens of thousands were in jail and it was not fashionable to ask the reason why. Cliches bounced off the tongues of the only people permitted to speak—spokesmen of the Congress, the CPI, and those who supported the Emergency.

There were times when I could have put my head in my hands and wept, that a nation accustomed to Jawaharlal Nehru's heart-searching and eloquence, a party once led by towering intellects, should now be at the mercy of a handful of mini-brains with three-and-a-half catch phrases between them in place of a vocabulary. Dictatorship, it was obvious, apart from its brutalities, was going to be excruciatingly boring. When "anti-fascist" conferences began to be held—with blood and thunder language used to describe these invisible (and as far as I could tell, non- existent) enemies of the people, Emergency language reached its peak of inanity. At the request of a lawyer friend in the Socialist Party I wrote a pamphlet for underground distribution, particularly at Patna, where the government was to hold a World Anti-Fascist Conference in December 1975. I quoted Nehru's speeches and writings to define fascism, and to point out that the definition squarely fitted the government in power. The pamphlet, I am told, flourished. Above ground my writing did not fare so well.

Everyman's had been shut down at the declaration of Emergency and Ajit Bhattacharjea, its editor, told me the police had shredded the last issue—an extraordinarily vindictive gesture, but in keeping with the fascist techniques used to intimidate all opposition. (Ajit had saved a copy of the last issues, and I promptly and lovingly laid all my issues, of *Everyman's* to rest in a safe place until they could surface again.) I could still write for the *Indian Express*, Editor-in-Chief, S. Mulgaokar told me, but not on any political subject. He was waiting himself to be told to leave and had stayed on this long only to help the owners over a difficult period.

I thought hard about a subject and came up with abortion. It is an important subject of course, and I had once been summoned by a Parliamentary committee to offer my views on it when legislation was being considered. But having contributed what understanding I could to the subject I had to think hard again about what to write next. One of the Shukla brothers had remarked with ill-concealed satisfaction to my mother at a wedding lunch we had all attended that now Nayantara would not be able to write about politics. My mother had retorted with her accustomed vigour that politics was not the only subject in the world, that civilized people had much else to talk and write about, and that her daughter, who was a novelist, had no dearth of topics to comment on. I tried to live up to this compliment and to be creative, but a ban on any side of creativity is a ban on all of it.

There is an indignity in being told virtually to shut up, which self-respecting people, especially those whose profession it is to think and write, find hard to accept. I kept thinking too, of the various ironies in this situation. My father Ranjit Sitaram Pandit, a Sanskrit scholar, a lover of languages, learning and literature, had cut these and much else that was dear to him out of his life when he joined the national movement, involving himself with politics and jail, because he had believed, like so many of his compatriots, that freedom came first. He had also believed his sacrifice would make it possible for future scholars and artists to do the work they loved best unharassed and in freedom.

My uncle Jawaharlal Nehru, a writer himself, had felt particularly tender toward the breed and had remained unshakable in his pledge that whatever Indians lacked, they would not lack freedom of expression, that there was no double standard of values—one for rich countries and another for the poor. There were some things that were the breath of life, and everyone needed them. I wondered what he would have thought of the Sahitya Akademi he had founded, unwilling now to utter even a sigh in protest. But I had a living to earn and I had to come up with a subject interesting enough for readers and innocuous enough for the censor. Reader-interest was an even more important consideration now that reading matter had become so dreary, and the speeches and public utterances we heard so repetitive. If one did not die of boredom, one might well go mad just listening to the sameness.

Newspapers had become a drag for it was news, above all, that was not available. One newspaper was too many to read when I had always read four. I wondered if the censor would object to adultery as a topic. Apparently he did not, and my next article was "Adultery in Life and Literature." It provoked Acharya Kripalani to the typical humorous retort in the press that he wished, he like Nayantara, could combat the woes of censorship through literary outlets of this sort. I did not see this remark when it was published, but he repeated it to me when we met in the corridors of the All India Medical Institute during JP's halt there in November 1975 on his way to hospital in Bombay. A knot of us, standing disconsolately about, were even able to laugh a little, and we needed to laugh in those days.

But soon my need to write what needed to be written was so overwhelming that my next two articles dealt with dissent in other times, and the atrocious punishments dealt out to those who had disobeyed authority. I recalled that one could be sentenced to death by poison for teaching the values of the good life, if these were different from what the state taught. One could be burned at the stake, broken on the wheel or condemned to the galleys for declaring, writing or printing "heresies" against the church or the monarch, or challenging current theories about the sun, the earth and the stars. From Socrates to Servetus and beyond prison torture or extermination had been ordinary matter-of-fact punishments for those who disagreed.

India was now adding a new chapter of her own to the record. I could not say so in so many words, but that was the inference—for I had a mounting horror of the Gulag Archipelago growing invisibly about us—the unnamed, unnumbered, unreported, undefended arrests, all the faceless multitude behind bars, in jails becoming monstrously overcrowded in the sweltering July-August-September heat of India. For the few who could eventually after much hardship, heartbreak, expense and red tape, be visited by their next of kin, there were thousands who could not. We do not know what these people suffered—the "average" citizen who was now the "average" prisoner—and how many of them fell ill, despaired or died. If people like himself, writers, journalists and other obstinate nuisances were intended to be in their number, the plan was obviously abandoned—though the threat continued—after Kuldip Nayar's arrest, which gave the regime a bad name and adverse publicity abroad.

Our tribe was, in any case, immobilized by censorship. Knowing my inability to stay immobilized very long, a Muslim friend whom I seldom saw as he was very much a pillar of the Establishment, took the trouble to toil up the two flights of stairs to my apartment in the furnace heat, to warn me to "lie low" as my comings and goings were watched and my telephone tapped. (Or did he say bugged? Anyway, the telephone was watching me, too.) I knew there was something odd going on, because on three occasions when I made a complaint about its functioning, the whole instrument was removed and changed. My friend said the awesome fact of power had to be recognised. The power set-up was here to stay. The sooner one bowed to it, the better. All resistance, he said, had been wiped out. It was no use hoping for a change.

Part of this was, no doubt, true. An American correspondent who had visited Bihar had told me that all traces of the Bihar Movement had been crushed like a cigarette butt under a boot, and by way of demonstration he had graphically ground his own heel into the carpet. But I knew that all resistance had not been wiped out. It never had, in any century, in any part of the world, under any sort of regime. The police state around us was evidence that it had not here. And if history teaches us anything, it is that power is never here to stay. I told my friend so and we had a futile quarrel, leaving us both angry and shaken. He departed on his well-intentioned round to warn others to "lie low," while I wondered how much damage he would succeed in doing by creating fear and bruising morale.

Earning a living was becoming more of a problem. Having commented obliquely on our "Gulag Archipelago" I could not think of one more thing to say for the newspapers. And my novel writing, which my mother had believed would save me from oblivion, presented its own difficulties. Now it was not a question of what was written, but who had written it. Dr. Lakshmi Narayan Lal, JP's Hindi biographer, who had discussed with me a Hindi translation by him of *The Day in Shadow*, told me the Hindi publisher found it unwise to produce my book at the present time. One publisher who had contracted to publish *A Situation in New Delhi*, apologized for not being able to do so and withdrew their contract. (If a contract is broken or nullified by circumstances beyond normal control—an act of God or State—I suppose there is nothing an author can do about it. I concluded that the overnight appearance of a dictatorship was such an act.) Another publisher, eager to pick up the option, also found it unsafe to handle, on the informal advice, they said, of someone in the censor's office.

Fiction often foreshadows fact. *The Day in Shadow* had had as an accompanying backdrop to Simrit's divorce settlement, the growing Soviet influence on our subcontinent and a definite Indian tilt in that direction. I finished writing the book in February 1971. The Indo-Soviet Treaty, a landmark of its kind, embodying this tilt, was not signed until August that year. The "situation" creeping upon us in *A Situation in New Delhi*—a book I had completed writing in January 1975—was upon us in June, and I myself was hung with it.

I went to see the Chief Censor. Harry D'Penha had been called out of retirement to handle this vital lever of dictatorship. He was cheerful and welcoming. In the past I had received the most courteous assistance from him when I had had occasion to seek special information. Harry advised me to wait till things eased up, if I had any doubts about my material. He also said the Home Ministry, not his department, handled books. He also expressed surprise that I should need advice about publishing. What could I have written that could not be published? Apparently there was one person in the land—and he, the Chief Censor—who did not know how the Establishment felt about me and how unacceptable my name and views were. Of course I did not go to the Home Ministry. There would have been no point unless I had changed my name on the manuscript to Susie Brown. I took my manuscript home and forgot about it. It had no importance now next to the sheer sickness I felt when I thought of admired, veteran leaders—some legendary for their contribution to India—in jail, of the many thousands with no famous name or background to protect them.

I had received from the P.E.N. in Bombay its resolution condemning censorship and had written to Madame Sophia Wadia congratulating the organization. It was the very least, I thought, that a writers' body could do. The previous year I had been invited to become a member of the Executive Committee of the newly set up Authors Guild of India, and had accepted. It seemed a worthwhile cause if it could help struggling authors with their publishing and other problems. I found, actually, that my presence on the committee, as indeed that of the other numbers, was superfluous. Justice G.D. Khosla, president, and D.R. Mankekar, general secretary conducted meetings between them with a very perfunctory attention to the others present. Both gentlemen were publicity-minded and, I felt, extremely anxious to be favourities at court. The plans they had for the Guild, it seemed to me, were heavily and needlessly dependent on the Government for favour, funds and patronage. The presence at the opening conference of the Guild of the Prime Minister, if possible, or another Minister, if necessary, was taken for granted. While this point appeared irrelevant to me in 1974, it appalled me in 1975. Representatives of a regime that stacked people into jail like last year's logs of firewood had no business, as far as I was concerned, on any respectable platform. I waited for some sign that the Guild would protest, not only against censorship, crippling to all real writing, but against imprisonment without trial, and would take up the cause of writers in prison.

Not a word was said about this, while a conference was busily planned for December with a Cabinet Minister presiding. I recommended we pass a resolution of the sort the P.E.N. had passed and gave

Mr. Mankekar a copy. I got no answer. The meeting went on as if nothing had happened. I thought the P.E.N. resolution, slipped into the general secretary's file, would be taken up at a later meeting. It was not. Neither the president nor the secretary made mention of it. I was deeply shocked by this attitude on the part of two men who profess to be concerned with human values. I resigned from the Guild's Executive Committee, succinctly stating my reasons in a correspondence with Mr. Mankekar. As I believed my resignation was not brought to the notice of the other members of the committee promptly, I put an advertisement in the *Indian Express* to this effect. In a dictatorship situation it is important to my mind, to be publicly clear-cut about one's beliefs if possible. For many people, whose dependents may suffer thereby, this is not possible. There were times, and this was one of them, when I felt I acted for those who wished to speak but could not. I was happy to note that a Guild member, Wing Commander S.N. Rampal, carried on a battle of his own with the Executive Committee about its conduct of Guild affairs, including the fact that my resignation and the reasons for it had not been put before the Guild. I had occasion to resign from the Sahitya Akademi's Advisory Board for English for the same reasons a few months later, in May 1976. I was asked not to press my resignation until the Akademi's Executive Board met to consider it. The meeting finally took place, I believe, in September 1976, when my resignation was accepted. This august body saw no reason either, it appears, to raise its voice on behalf of freedom.

I looked around at the debris of the vigorous, independent penmanship of which India had been justly proud. Respected editors and journalists were out of jobs, or making do with what they could find. Sycophancy had grown to fantastic proportions. I had already stopped my subscription to the *Hindustan Times* and the *Illustrated Weekly of India*, some of whose classic issues will, I hope, be preserved as museum pieces. Meeting friends was something of a relief, but even a social gathering was distressing when "walls had ears" and conversation had to be guarded.

Yet parties were the only source of stray fragments of real news, and one clung to the fragments one got. Sometimes parties became strained and tense too. At the home of a friend I had a fierce argument with a Congress Member of Parliament, whose argument suddenly collapsed with the pathetic statement that it would take the next generation, trained in subversion and firearms, to overthrow the present setup in the Congress and the country. It struck me that an M.P. who could in desperation speak this way of his party and the condition it had brought about, yet with no will to act against it, did indeed belong to its last gasp. And I was more convinced than ever that the shadow of defeat lay over the Congress, and the power structure, ostensibly invulnerable, was hollow within. But things might go on this way for months and years, a waste of time that could be spent usefully somewhere else. And I gratefully accepted an opportunity to go to the United States on a six month research scholarship at the Radcliffe Institute. I remained abroad until August 1977, writing and teaching, first in Cambridge, Massachusetts where I worked on a book, and later at Southern Methodist University in Dallas, Texas, where as writer-in-residence I led two seminars in Creative Writing. My stay abroad gave me the opportunity to try to acquaint Americans with events in India. The contents of this book (*A Voice for Freedom*), except for an article I wrote for the *Times* (London), are the result of my endeavours.

I acknowledged authorship of an article I wrote for the *New Republic* under the pseudonym Azad when Leila Fernandes, in exile with her son, and tormented with anxiety about her husband, asked me if she could use my name in her statement in Washington before a committee of Congress for international relations. The Indian embassy in Washington sent a senior diplomat, Mr. Inam Rahman, to my seminar at the Radcliffe Institute in November 1976, and a month later Mr. Janaki Butt of the India Consulate General in New York attended my talk at Columbia University. Neither attempted conversation with me. I suppose you do not chat pleasantly with a thorn in your side.

My activities were reported home, but they could have carried no surprises for new Delhi. Officialdom would perhaps have found it more instructive to attend an evening gathering at the home of my valued friend, longtime friend of India, and a staunch supporter of all good human causes, Dorothy Norman. I had, with her permission, invited Subramaniam Swamy, on the run from the Indian authorities at the time. After somewhat conventional talks providing the background and meaning of the Emergency by Rajni Kothari, Ved Mehta and myself, Swamy's down-to-earth remarks, crisply delivered with no ifs, buts or frills, had a tonic effect on the audience representing important human rights organisations, the P.E.N., and distinguished academics, journalists and others interested in Indian developments. The last things that many present expected of a Jana Sangh was that he would be a modern, articulate, Harvard educated economist, with a practical knowledge of the Indian countryside and a lively sense of humour.

"People need to know," I told Swamy afterward, "that the Jana Sangh does not have three horns and a tail." What I meant was that it was time people took another look at India. Three months later, after the March election, they did.

A Miscellany

A Tribute to the Punjab*

Winter is a treat anywhere in North India. In Chandigarh it is especially lovely. I walk through fields that undulate toward low, mist-covered hills, and the ground is at times caked hard beneath my feet where the water course has dried long since, at times soft and sinking where a villager's bicycles has driven deep grooves into the dusty path. The lake looks pliable and metallic reflecting the copper glow of the late sun. This calm landscape carries no reminders of the recent conflict with Pakistan, nor was Chandigarh directly involved in it, not coming under enemy fire or bearing the brunt of the bombs as did other parts of the state. Yet it is the capital, and symbolic in ways both human and architectural, of a Punjab that emerged with a renewed and robust vitality after the Partition. Looking at the comparative prosperity of this state it is hard to believe that these were the people who eighteen years ago trekked in blood and tatters to an uncertain future, often leaving the ruin of a lifetime's labour and industry behind them, these the people who set to work with no self-pity to plough fresh fields, build new industries and shoulder new burdens, many of them at a time of life when beginnings could not have been easy. And more recently these were the people who sprang to attention, marshalled their resources with lightning rapidity and mobilized to a man, without a whimper, when last September's conflict burst upon them. The fields during those months of crisis were astir with vigilant kisans out with their lathis in search of paratroopers. The highways remained busy thoroughfares and buses continued to ply their routes in spite of air raids. Women brought hot meals to the jawans on their way to and from the battlefronts and everywhere tea and cigarettes were served free to the fighting man. There was no panic in the Punjab. The day's work went on, backed by the dogged determination to see that chapter through. Now, walking through the serene countryside, watching peasants coax their cattle homeward, talking gently to them, nudging them along as if they were sleepy children, I have wondered about

* *The Sunday Standard*, 9 January 1966

that determined spirit, so distinct in its manifestations from the tone and temper found in the rest of India.

Part of its energy is that it brooks no compromise. Yet I have always considered this something of a paradox in people who live among so much abundance and who dispense it so freely in their daily lives and contacts. I have associated the stark regions of the globe with the uncompromising spirit—the North West Frontier, the steppes of Soviet Asia, the wastelands and the deserts where the earth does not yield even its scant reward without a struggle, where men must toil incessantly and have little time for the tranquil pursuits, where bare hills, slate skies and a leaden austerity rule stretches of stony soil. If civilization, as Will Durand says, is a union of soil and soul, then the hardships imposed by bleak and barren soil would naturally produce strongly delineated character, where issues would be black and white, right and wrong, good and evil, and the softer hues of compromise would not exist. That would be the climate and the geography to sustain old feuds and kindle vendettas. But what had such rigidity of outlook to do with the Punjab in all its sleek abundance, blessed as it was with man and nature's bounty? "Nigh," a friend told me, was the Punjabi word that best described the quality of friendliness and generosity found here, a word as familiar as the "razai" used in winter, and generating much of the same warmth.

One explanation of this paradox might be that these are a people who have had an unbroken and healthy tradition of land ownership, deriving their confidence from their pride of possession. The long held dogma, like the belief in the strong right arm, prospers in such an atmosphere. Britain's ninety-year contact with the Punjab did little to alter or diminish the relationship between the Punjabi farmer or landowner and his acres. In contrast Britain's 300-year rule over Bengal transformed and impoverished its agriculture and crippled its rural economy in the first heady flush of empire-building. In Bengal the British found human material with which they could experiment, laying the foundations of a revolution in education and outlook. Bengal was their laboratory. In the Punjab they stopped short, not only because it was the last, geographically, of their conquests in India, but because here they encountered a resistance they recognized and respected, a spirit very akin to their own in its tenacity. It is a spirit that will triumph in wars, and in peacetime will flourish in town and countryside. Its possessors will work hard and wholeheartedly enjoy the fruits of their enterprise. The only thing they lack, if it can be called a lack, is a wistfulness—the feeling that when the day's task is well and manfully done, the family fed and the fires out for the night, there is still much left unanswered.

Heroes and Hysteria*

All the world loves a lover, and every Indian, it seems, loves a hero, with this difference that the hero he loves has to belong to his own particular region. He wants to be certain to keep his enthusiasm and admiration within bounds—and boundaries—and not be carried away by just any hero. His own special hero has to be one who was born in his own state. What would he want with someone born fifty or a few hundred miles away? He may be a thoroughly nice chap, but a foreigner after all and therefore to be kept in his place—in the neighbouring state.

The Greeks defined a hero as any free man (in a society that was divided into slaves and free men) who took his own part in the Trojan War and about whom a story could be told. According to this definition of achievement in battle, heroism has abounded in Indian history. Maharashtra, Rajasthan and the plains of North India have been the scene of a glittering array of valiant deeds. Perhaps the very size of this spectacle is so dazzling that we want to keep our heroes in little compartments for local consumption only.

I became conscious of the cult of the hero and the growing majesty of the state when I came to live in Maharashtra. I was aware, of course, that India meant diversity, a rich and varied mosaic every Indian had in the past accepted with matter-of-factness and even with humour. Perhaps no state illustrated this variety better than Uttar Pradesh, which had a population of residents from all over the country, many of whom had lived there for several generations without ever giving up an infinitesimal fraction of their own way of living, eating and speaking toward a common culture. The Bengalis, the Malabaris and the Kashmiris in Uttar Pradesh all remained dedicatedly Bengali, Malabari and Kashmiri. No Kashmiri family ever thought of serving rasam for dinner one day along with the pulao and koftas, and no Malabari housewife would have dreamed of learning to make a Kashmiri dish. The idea would have been quite revolutionary had it ever occurred to anyone. It

* *The Sunday Standard*, 3 July 1966

never did. And the orthodox Bengali housewife remained an orthodox Bengali. She always wore her sari in the traditional way with her keys tied to the end of it and slung over her shoulder and never, never felt like dressing differently for a change on Saturdays. And this had gone on since time immemorial and it would go on forever more. Everyone lived happily in the same province and minded their own business. Occasionally freaks inter-married and people were aghast for a little while, but whatever happened nobody hit his neighbour on the head, shouted himself hoarse or held up a train.

Now for the first time, living in Maharashtra during the language agitation, I felt a sinister note had crept into what had been a happy diversity. There were language riots, an ugly tug-of-war over the future of Bombay city, and finally the triumphant inauguration of the new state of Maharashtra. At midnight on the first of May 1960, at a distinguished function on the lawns of Raj Bhavan, a curtain was drawn aside to the sound of conch shells and the tinkling of bells to reveal a map, not of India containing the new state of Maharashtra, but an isolated map of Maharashtra outlined in electric lights, shorn of the country in which it was situated. Since one does not recognize the outline of each state in isolation, it looked unfamiliar. It took a minute to realize what it represented. It might have been Timbuctoo. However, it was not. It was Maharashtra, retaining its capital, Bombay, after some gory street rioting. It had its own batch of "martyrs," men who had been needlessly sacrificed to the whim of local politicians in a bloody street incident, and who would have served their country and their state better alive than in the senseless agitation that brought about their untimely end. And it was proposed to commemorate these poor misguided dead by erecting a statue on a remarkably ugly pedestal at Flora Fountain, where aesthetics demanded no second statue should be. But that was not the end of it. The new state had to have a symbol and so it resurrected the image of Shivaji, and what had been a brilliant historical memory to thrill and delight any school-going child and give him a pride in his heritage, became a tedious cult. Not one, I am certain, would have objected to it more strenuously than Shivaji himself, too dynamic, daredevil and romantic a figure to wish to become a bore.

It is always useful when everyone stands up and cheers, to find out exactly what they are cheering about before one joins in the celebration. So what was all the cheering about, I wondered? Why had the unveiling of an illuminated, unrecognizable map at midnight, and the decision to put up a sad-looking statue in quite a presentable area of Bombay generated a peculiar and frightening new trend that would have resembled nationalism had Maharashtra been a nation? And if it was not a nation, why did it make noises like one? I examined my own ancestry, which was half Maharashtrian, to try and locate an upsurge of feeling, some echo that would rise up and quiver with excitement at the new developments, but there was none. I only felt a vague irritation that adults should behave in this excitable manner over a piece of territory which, give or take a few square miles, was still a part of India, always had been, and God willing, always would be.

Nor did I feel like growing emotional over Shivaji. This man who had become a legend in his own lifetime was probably one of the most attractive personalities in any country's history. But the mention of his name did not make me want to brandish a sword against my neighbour. It might have if this had been the seventeenth century and Maratha territory struggling for survival against a hostile empire. But it wasn't the seventeenth century any more and Shivaji needed to be seen in perspective: only a hundred years before him Akbar had united a large part of India into a single empire and ruled it with a vision of human brotherhood far ahead of his era. This grand achievement was speedily disposed of by Aurangzeb and Shivaji who between them—albeit at odds with each other—hastened the end of Akbar's empire and his dream of the unity of India. Of course they had their reasons. Aurangzeb wanted a Muslim India while Shivaji ignited a militant Hindu nationalism. And neither was the statesman Akbar was. And that is all, briefly, that can be said about that particular chapter.

There's nothing wrong with heroes so long as we don't get hysterical about them.

Anything Goes*

Suddenly it's over. The steam of vitality that was frothing and bubbling out of Czechoslovakia has been checked. A stone has been laid at its mouth, the chinks and gaps rigorously cemented. From now on the water will trickle obediently from under the stone, in measured quantity, with no embarrassing outbursts of spontaneity, and there will be no sparkling torrent of a people's adventure in self-expression to infect and enthuse their iron-clad environs.

From the pathos of the Czech drama, from its brevity, and above all from its sinister noiselessness—hardly a shot fired—one is reminded of the tremendous power and authority of the Soviet machine in Eastern Europe, its relentless hold upon its bloc, and of the violence that is a continual menacing presence in the air. The most heroic of men and women—and the Czechs certainly qualify for heroism—cannot argue with tanks and machine guns. Nor can a tiny country the size of Czechoslovakia, and with its geographical position, opt to be wiped out in any lone suicidal resistance to the Russians. If Mr. Dubcek gave his consent to the Moscow agreement there was nothing else he could do.

It is over and the shock of it has been felt around the world. A grim conclusion emerges from these events, that violence is a persistent and often a successful factor in international politics. Violence works, and no one can interfere with its working. It does not even have to be explained any more. Any flimsy excuse will serve to justify it, even that the Soviet invasion was "invited" by the Czechs. We have swallowed some tall stories in our time but this is really too much. It would have been more in line with brutal aggression to give no excuse at all. The current Soviet violence has not even had the universal support of Communist parties in other countries. Only seven of the world's ninety Communist parties (apart from the invading five themselves) supported the invasion. And nobody knows—or will ever know—whether the citizens of the invading powers backed it, or whether protests against it were quickly and efficiently silenced.

---

* *The Sunday Standard*, 15 September 1968

The Russians have made nonsense even of their own Warsaw Treaty declaration. According to the Treaty the parties undertook to refrain from the threat or use of force in their international relations and to settle all disputes by peaceful means. All that went up in Soviet smoke when the Warsaw powers rolled into Czechoslovakia. The upshot is that apparently foreign—albeit "allied"—armies can occupy your soil overnight, and the world will shed tears for you but it will not be able to lift a little finger to help you sign an "agreement" at gun point and the freedom of your children is amputated for another generation.

How far humanity has travelled in cynicism since the revulsion and recoil from violence that followed the First World War. Not that we have not tried to set up sanctions against it, but the sanctions have been moral, and morality has a long way to go to catch up with power politics. The U.N. is there and we thank God for it, but it is rather like a parent who loves you, yet is helpless to shelter you from life's more vicious blows. Today though we still cry out against violence, we accept it. We bow to the fact that it exists in the world's body politic, in the scheme of things, in the state of affairs known as Balance of Power which divides the world into armed camps and spheres of influence. When a powder keg blows up in one camp, it is politic to hold your peace, not ask too many questions, and convey your sympathy to the bleeding victims in cautious tones lest it blow up in your own backyard next. What use has the paralyzed world been to Czechoslovakia, beyond its righteous expressions of shock? What use has America been, guilt-ridden with Viet Nam? Its impotence has in fact made the criminality of the Super-Power system more apparent than ever: "You stay out of my yard and I'll stay out of yours." What use have Britain and France been, preoccupied with their own internal problems, or the countries of Asia and Africa, bewildered about the implications of being friends with the Soviet Union? Even we in India, with our passionate sympathy for the Czechs in their travail, must needs hold our tongue at Government level for the sake of the Soviet veto in the Security Council over Kashmir. For various reasons we have all remained merely stricken spectators. We might as well not have been there. It's a long time since the nineteen thirties when anguished young men of different nations joined the International Brigade to fight fascism in Spain.

And what has happened in India to the Soviet image during this brief nightmare? It was already beginning to tarnish a little with the announcement of Soviety military aid to Pakistan. With the attack on Czechoslovakia, years of friendliness and a growing confidence in the Soviet bona fides have been rudely shaken. It seems incredible stupidity on the part of the Soviets to take a step that so deliberately turns back the clock in international understanding and so nakedly shows up the strong arm method they use to get their way. We will go on doing business with the Soviet Union because it is to our mutual advantage to do so, but the Indian people do not like bullies, whatever their geographical or ideological position.

Twenty years ago we decided not to join any power bloc but to be part of a "third area" for peace. The outcome of the Czech crisis—which has revealed the moral indefensibility and actual impotence of the Super Power system—has vindicated that stand. In 1947 we were new on the world stage and somewhat starry-eyed. We are of age now and the only thing we have to ensure, reference others, is our capacity to defend ourselves. Independence has no other meaning.

Drinking—Indian Style*

I don't hold with prohibition. It has done us irreparable harm in creating a contempt for the law. It has cost us lakhs we can ill afford to spend on the cumbersome machinery required to enforce it. And it has failed. The manufacture of illicit liquor has become a cottage industry, and a new business, bootlegging, flourishes. Be that as it may, I wish with a passion that Indians would not drink. They don't know how to. This is one Western custom that has not exported well. Consider the way we serve and imbibe alcohol as compared with our Western counterparts.

In Europe wine is served as an accompaniment to food. In England it is customary to serve a drink, perhaps two, to guests before a meal. Nobody settles down to a long drinking session before eating. If it's a long session he wants he goes to a pub. At a party guests will generally remain standing and move in to lunch or dinner, all their faculties in good repair, within half an hour of their arrival—and they will arrive on time. Look what happens here. Time being of no consequence, people arrive any time they want to, even an hour after the time stated on the invitation. Not that it matters, and neither host nor guest is the least dismayed, as dinner won't be served for another couple of hours. The pattern of such a party is predictable. Round after round of liquor, apart from making the party noisier, does little else. No one is wittier or more scintillating because of drink. The whole business becomes mechanical, the regular replacement of an empty glass for a full one. No one thinks of saying No. Very often there is a knot of tired, resigned women on the outskirts of the group, patiently waiting for the food to be served and the evening to be over. They just have to wait.

I've waited myself, at times with a keyed-up curiosity to see which side will hold out longer. Will the host surrender first and stop the steady flow, or will the guests have the eccentricity to refuse the next drink and a general slump in the imbibing pace compel the ordering of dinner? The guests have so far won every encounter. There are always

---

* *The Sunday Standard*, 29 January 1969

some still drinking, no matter what time dinner is announced. A point the host must consider, I suppose, is his reputation. How will the poor man hold up his head in public if he announces dinner at a reasonable hour? After all, people can dine at that hour in their own homes any day of the week. When they go out, they *expect* to booze. Except for the dowry system, nowhere has "face" mattered more. Under Indian management the cocktail hour has become the cocktail three-hour.

Unable to understand this kind of entertaining. I have thought of a remedy which might charitably be put into effect for the benefit of sufferers like myself. Instead of inviting guests at a particular hour, the host could state the time at which dinner will be served. The evening then need not become a protracted burden to those who do not drink, and these people would be free to spend the earlier part of the evening at home. Instead of watching people get steadily inebriated for two hours, I, for instance, could be with my daughter while she has her dinner, catch up with my housekeeping, read a book, write an article or just relax. I do object to my time being requisitioned to no purpose. The other possibility of course, is to take some knitting along to the party, but I have refrained for fear of causing offence.

I am strongly prejudiced perhaps by my background. I grew up in a home where nothing stronger than tomato juice was ever served. And it was a home where talk was lively and living had sparkle. There was never a dull moment. No one needed a whiskey in order to produce an anecdote or an idea. I went to an American mission school (part of our boycott of British institutions at the time) run by another extraordinarily dedicated group of people. They were men and women who believed in what they were doing and conveyed that belief to every child in their care with both vigour and humour. Again, they were people who flourished without alcohol and everything around them flourished. It brings me to the conclusion that people with an objective, people living for something, going toward something, do not need either an escape or a crutch of any kind. Of course there are awfully grim dull types who are dedicated, too, but in my experience the person with a star to follow is seldom dull and has a tremendous buoyancy and gaiety of spirit that needs nothing artificial to bolster it.

The confirmed drinkers perpetuate a lot of myths about alcohol: "Most drinkers are fine chaps." "X is so much more charming when he has had a few." "It's really good for one, in moderation." Moderation is never defined. It can't be. It has to be a very flexible word to accommodate as much as the drinker thinks he can hold. And I suppose there must be as many fine chaps who don't drink as do. As for X being charming after a few, he is nothing of the sort. Usually he is repetitive.

According to what the brew brings out in him he may become aggressive or lascivious. He may even fall asleep in the soup. I have failed, I must confess, to discover added charm from a bottled source. A continual discovery, on the other hand, is that my countrymen don't know when to stop. "Oh, but he wasn't drunk. He never raised his voice" is probably the most dangerous myth of all. You can be well and truly drunk without ever raising your voice in an argument or a quarrel. You can just get vague looking and stupid instead, with slower reflexes, as if the fatigue of the ages had caught up with you.

It is a pity we confuse the issue of drinking with morality. It is not an evil the way prohibitionists here look at it. It is, in quantity, a poison—and that should be sufficient reason for any sensible person to keep off it. But long before it becomes a poison in the body, it is a nuisance and a bore. It drags a party on intolerably and makes nonsense of the reason why people should get together, which is the desire for company and conversation. I think we'd do much better to stick to "lassi."

Intellectual Giant of the Century*

There are men who one forgets are mortal, who arouse our anger when they die, whose contribution to the world is so many-sided, increasing so phenomenally in its sweep and scope as time goes on, that they have no business to die. We do not accept their death.

Bertrand Russell was the great result, perhaps the greatest in his own long lifetime, of what a civilization in which free speculation is possible, can produce. Civilization has a long history and many shades of meaning, but there is one attribute without which it cannot be so-called: that is the climate which makes possible the life of the mind. There have been remarkable intellects, but few in any age like Russell's, which refused to be awed by anything under the sun.

When a mind of this dimension is involved with the suffering and savagery of its times and joins battle with them, the result is something titanic, almost beyond human proportion. Russell's life assumed this stature in his later years when he fought with all the knowledge and persuasion in his possession to warn mankind that nuclear destruction was no vague distant threat but a present, actual terror. Yet pacifist was a singular misnomer for the unrelenting war he waged on so many fronts against the lack or the miscarriage of justice. And to call him a mathematician or a philosopher was never enough. What Russell gave the world was more than original thinking in mathematics and philosophy. He provided us with the astonishing and poignant spectacle over the space of nearly a century of a man who strove with his whole being to overcome in his personal relationships the painful barriers of personality, and at the public level perpetually to re-state and re-enforce his links with humanity. What man strove for, he said, was "some kind of struggling emergence of mind"—the slow and steady additional achievement that is every generation's legacy to the next and which is the journey we call civilization.

In his own career there were two aspects to this human advance.

---

* *The Sunday Standard*, 15 February 1970

One was the pursuit of pure knowledge, and he delved deep into his own branches of knowledge in search of exactitude and truth. The other was that, if thought is man's highest achievement, then it must enter the arena to deal with practical problems. He poured the results of his own thinking on many subjects—philosophical, scientific, political, educational and moral—into more than fifty publications, in lucid, impeccable prose that any man who reads and thinks can enjoy, and became known through these to millions the world over whom pure science and philosophy neither reach nor touch. Philosophy he once defined as teaching man "how to live without certainty and yet without being paralyzed by hesitation." There was no better example than his own life, for he plunged into active demonstration of what he stood for whenever he could, as in the case of the school he and his wife Dora started because they found established education unsatisfactory; and his participation, even at the age of ninety, in public protests against the Vietnam war and nuclear weapons. He was in this respect what few men have been, a carrier of culture, who put his ideas to work in an impressive variety of programmes and issues. From his own personal development to a deep involvement with other people's pain, there was not one flagging moment when his reliance on reason or his convictions failed him. And to the end, in spite of his disappointment and disillusionment with the progress of his fight for nuclear disarmament, he believed in the possibility of a golden age, provided man would make up his mind to choose life, not death.

There was almost no established belief he did not question. A member of the aristocracy, he gave up his inheritance. Born and educated during the Victorian era he was nevertheless, as a result of his unorthodox upbringing, non-conformist to the marrow, beginning with his surprise at the age of eleven on discovering that Euclid's geometrical axioms had to be accepted without proof, and going on to his espousal of the free trade movement, women's suffrage, his conscientious objection during the First World War, and causes as far flung as India's independence, the truth about President Kennedy's assassination and the treatment of Jews in Soviet Russia. He expressed himself bluntly on nearly every important issue of his day and made history because he practised what he believed, from his undaunted search for the honest and loving relationship in marriage to his strenuous commitment to peace—based on so startling a concept as the utter unimportance of nationhood and national prestige as compared with the survival of the human species and its total achievement. Perhaps no scientist and no philosopher ever had as much to do with life and the living.

Russell was too big for his times, too undivided an integrity for the comfort of any Establishment, not to become the target of all kinds of attack, personal and political. He refused to follow any dictate but that of scientific intelligence. Morality for him began with that. He endured imprisonment and ridicule in his own country and vituperation in the United States. There is hardly anything so extraordinary as the witch hunt to which America subjected him because of his views, until the McCarthy witch hunt against Americans began. Through it all his career went on inexorably as the ocean, with something of the ocean's grandeur. His autobiography written in beautiful, often moving language, reveals a life fully and closely examined, showing the naked progress of his searches and what they meant to him.

I wonder if this is still the kind of world that can produce men like Russell. It is, first of all, increasingly the world of the specialist, in which knowledge is narrowed down more and more, almost shutting out the larger vision. It is also the world of the technician, the man with the know-how, the formula rather than the field from which it springs. The specialist and the technician, brilliant in their own departments, are apt to be lost outside these.

Then, in the last forty years or so there has been a definite authoritarian trend over a large part of the world: the Communist Revolution with its capture of Central Europe and China, dictators in Italy and Germany, and the dictatorships that still flourish in Spain, Portugal and many parts of Latin America. These are, or have been, areas where the exercise of personality and free speculation are not possible. Where the State or the Leader is god, there are distinct limits to how far and in what direction man may go. The mind of man in vast areas has thus never operated under so many confines as it does in this century we think of as progressive. This is quite a sobering thought. And there seems to be no possibility in the foreseeable future of this picture changing.

It was once believed that the "thaw" in the Soviet Union would produce a springtime which would set free the mind, now that the basic needs of the people—food, shelter, education—had been supplied through untold hardship and sacrifice, and world power status achieved. But that is not so. The Czechoslovak crisis proved it was not so. Events in the Soviet Union itself, with the periodic rounding up of dissenters, confirms it. We have to come to the conclusion that there is no link, no possible connection between authoritarianism and freedom. The one has to be destroyed in order to achieve the other. Neither can grow in the normal course out of the other. It is hard to see, therefore, how the spirit of man can grow wings and soar in climes such as these, deadening in the extreme.

There is also very much with us the poverty and struggle of non-Comunist Asia where basic needs are yet to be supplied, and which may in this decade tilt in an increasingly authoritarian direction to find its answers. If this happens there will be less and less scope for individual development. Even today we in India with our freedoms still intact, are caught in traps from which we find it difficult to escape, chiefly the huge and growing population whose needs no successes in field and factory can cope with. Above all, can education have any meaning in this situation of swelling numbers, poorly paid teachers, ill-prepared students concerned about their future livelihood? Where, in all this, is there the possibility of training the mind, encouraging the growth of ideas? In fact, if we try to discover what India gave to civilization we have to go back to 500 B.C. It is a question mark whether we will, in fact, be able by some miracle to get through the next decades peacefully and in freedom. Until that happens we will have only the ghosts of such men as Russell among us, voices from the past to remind us that where men are at liberty to think there is hardly any limit to what man's mind can encompass and produce to enrich and comfort all men on earth.

The Tragedy of America*

Power politics never present an edifying moral spectacle. Most moral values get trampled in the game of power. Yet seldom has there been such an astoundingly brutal burial of morality by power as in the American Government's posture in the present crisis on this subcontinent. Or perhaps we feel stunned by its posture because no matter what has happened in the past, no matter what the continuing evidence, we continue to expect a modicum of morality from America.

It should have been abundantly clear by now that "the land of the free and the home of the brave" does not countenance freedom and bravery anywhere else in the world. We have watched this unhappy development ever since America assumed its Great Power role after the Second World War. We had not expected the kind of development that took place. Roosevelt had been a champion of India's struggle for freedom. He had sent emissaries to the leaders of the national movement and interceded with Churchill for a speedy transfer of power. But the war ended, Roosevelt died, and no one of his vision or calibre took his place. A new era began for the United States based on an overriding hysteria against Communism that seemed to blot out plain common sense, much less permit the Government to formulate a mature and realistic foreign policy. Externally the administration cut itself off from all communication with one of the gigantic actualities of the post-war scene—the People's Republic of China—adamantly opposing its entry into the U.N. Internally it gave its support to McCarthy's assault on civil liberties, exposing its own citizens to a frightening witch hunt that even its large and distinguished community of liberals and intellectuals could do little to combat. Never had a great nation so completely lost its nerve and its poise. No wonder its Asia policy stemmed from wrong premises and led to strange results, for it had failed to grasp the major reality of the mid-twentieth century, which was not the bogey of Communism but the end of colonial empires and the emergence of the national aspira-

---

* *The Sunday Standard*, 26 December 1971

tions of hundreds of millions of Asians. No wonder it saw the world in terms of its own formula, forgetting that the world outside the United States is an ancient one and that there are human and historic urges within it that do not obey any pat formula.

So America missed the bus in Asia. It propped up the dictators. It threw the weight of its official support and sympathy behind corrupt regimes that did not have the backing of their people. It mistook the huge nationalist upheaval in Viet Nam for a Communist versus anti-Communist war. It poured money and arms into Formosa to create a new pawn in the international power game which it has now abruptly and ruthlessly repudiated. On this subcontinent it found it politic to bolster a military dictatorship in Pakistan and support its odyssey of fanaticism rather than back the bravest experiment in democracy the world has ever seen. America could not back India because America demanded allegiance to its formula. To be considered America's friend one had to enter its pacts, join its military lineup. "You are either for us or against us" was the refrain that symbolized the nightmarish Dullesian delusion on which American policy in Asia was based, and it was assuredly a nightmare for people who were neither for nor against anybody, who wanted the goodwill and support of all the Powers, big and small, in order to be able to build in freedom.

India was accused over the years of moralizing, of having a holier than thou attitude, of non-alignment inclining toward the Soviet Union. Fair enough. There may have been much justice in the criticisms levelled against us. We were certainly made fully aware on every possible occasion of how imperfect, how impossible we were. But it occurred to us to wonder, too, how a foreign policy so misguided, so inept, and so totally cynical could issue from America? Human rights, the passion to be free, the belief that all men everywhere should be free, were ideals the world's people had associated with America. We in India had borrowed from the American Constitution. Lincoln and Jefferson belonged to us. In our poverty, and up against problems that almost defied solution, we dared to choose America's way of life, with its profound respect for the individual, its faith in government by choice. We believed mistakenly, that this was an act of courage, almost of prayer that would be understood above all, by America. It was not, for there was no link between what America believed, the things it taught its children, and the way it acted. And over the years it became apparent that whatever terrible damage this breach between belief and action did in Asia, it was as nothing compared with the damage it did to Americans, going against the very bloodstream of thinking Americans. More and more they found themselves up against a situation they could not stomach, could not square with their consciences.

Policies alter and even change, as they must to suit new historical circumstances. But never has any policy so totally acknowledged its own defeat as the volte face of America on China. Twenty years earlier the recognition of China would have been wholly right. Today it solves only half the problem. It is still correct, but in these twenty years China's isolation has made it a hard and bitter bargainer. The earth's most ancient pragmatists will squeeze every advantage out of America's late awakening to reality, and the countries of Asia may well be the losers in the shadow of this long-delayed event. The pull-out from Viet Nam is another self-confessed failure of policy, one that leaves behind it a sickening residue of human and material waste. And at the tail end of the long muddle—one might call it the most deplorable stroke of the policymakers' brush—comes the American Government's refusal to raise even a murmur against Yahya Khan for his well-thought-out butchery in Bangla Desh, resulting in the biggest refugee migration known to history. Far from facing facts America is now trying to legitimize this horror through the U.N. Could even power politics reach a more refined pinnacle of cynicism?

We are told that the American swing toward China shows Mr. Nixon's new realism. But he has understood only one half of Asia's reality. China is that half. The other half is India. For these two very different countries with their utterly dissimilar traditions and national characters are both Asia's authentic voices, and any Big Power dabbling in Asia will sooner than later have to come to grips with this fact. The macabre aspect of American policy is that while it has at last accepted the fact that the Chinese had the right to over-throw their government by revolutionary methods and establish a new system within their borders, it has never appreciated the much simpler phenomenon that there exists in Asia a country with ideals similar to America's that has laboured to bring about change democratically, and has nurtured civilized practices in its relationship with other nations. Perhaps it is too simple a fact to grasp. Perhaps Mr. Nixon will wake up to it eventually—but what unimaginable damage he may have done by then.

There is tragedy enough in the situation we face, with an overwhelming load of human misery still on our hands—though the refugees are now beginning to return—and a war we had no alternative but to fight. But the fundamental tragedy may well be America's, who has deliberately chosen to ignore the reason why nine million men, women and children crossed the border into India. No one leaves his home unless he is driven from it, unless the terror, torture and humilitation unleashed on him become too much to bear. To the brutal reason behind this exodus and therefore to the truth of the matter America has closed its eyes. We can only weep for a country that has so deserted its past, forgotten so utterly that it came into being when its forefathers decided they would not submit to persecution, and that whatever the cost, they would create a nation and a society where men could live in self-respect.

There is an additional irony in America's backing of the military junta in West Pakistan, for the people of West Pakistan are not likely to support it very long themselves. It is inconceivable that decent people anywhere can, once they know the facts, support a saga of such savagery as was practised on Bangla Desh.

As for ourselves, twenty-four years of growth in freedom, of government by choice, have given us a confidence not easy to intimidate or destroy. Another point not fully understood by the outsider is that India is undeniably a nation—intensely individualistic and argumentative within its borders and over internal issues, but single-minded and united in the face of any outer threat. The struggle to do without—if America withdraws aid—may be hard but it may be the crowning of our independent nationhood. The capacity of our civilization and its values to survive is one of the puzzles of history. Now we shall do much more than survive. We shall celebrate that survival in every corner of this country, knowing that our own strength and effort must ensure that our way of life continues in freedom.

Nabokov Remembered*

It was not, and still is not, the practice for a teacher to introduce his own accomplishment to a new class, or we would have known, the September day in 1945 when Vladimir Nabokov** walked in, that he was the author of a series of outstanding novels in Russian, that the *New Yorker, Harper's* and *Atlantic Monthly* were publishing his English stories, and critics were celebrating their discovery of a genius. Edmund Wilson, then or soon afterward, called him "the most extraordinary phenomenon of the kind since Conrad . . . something like Proust, something like Franz Kafka, and probably, something like Gogol . . . (but) as completely himself as any of these other writers." Enough and to spare for conceit, and we, with a year or more at Wellesley College in Massachusetts behind us, were quick to detect it where we found it in our teachers. A narcissistic entrant to the philosophy faculty was known among his students as "God's gift to the Greeks" since he clearly believed that was what he was. If there was any trace of conceit about Mr. Nabokov, we never saw it.

All I knew when he walked in was that his appearance—long, lean and balding, his shoulders slightly raised, slightly hunched, the way he wore his clothes, rather loosely—all in some indefinable way said "European." He must have been forty-six years old. The American world around me was new, young, untarnished, measurable in decades. Since my arrival in America a year earlier, the beauty and serenity of Wellesley had seemed almost unbelievable against the war news from Europe and Asia, and the imprisoned parents, fighting for freedom, I had left at home. The war had just barely ended, but my father had died of his prison term, and freedom for India was still not in sight. There were times when Wellesley's inhabitants and their concerns looked ex-

---

* *Span*, February 1978

** The recent death of Vladimir Nabokov evokes memories in an Indian writer of the days when, at a college in Massachusetts, Nabokov unveiled the mysteries of the Russian language in beautifully precise English, re-creating the setting of Tsarist Russia with remarkable clarity.

quisitely unreal to me. Instinctively I reached out for the anchor of older experience, and was consoled by maturity where I found it, more often in my books and teachers than in my fellow students. I thought Mr. Nabokov handsome. It would have been a wildly improbable thing to say in a teen-age environment where handsomeness was crew-cut, up-turned-nosed, suitably muscular, in or just out of uniform, always and invariably young, and preferably marriageable. So I didn't say it.

We sat, fifteen or twenty of us—a lot for a language class, and Russian at that—at a long table, and after the preliminaries Mr. Nabokov walked to the blackboard—we discovered he almost never sat down—and wrote on it in English script the Russian word "kneega." He said the word lingeringly out loud, and asked us to repeat it several times. "Do you *like* it?" he demanded, "Is it *pleasing* to you?" It meant, we learned, book. We learned more than its meaning. It taught us to join two consonants, an exercise alien to the Anglo-Saxon tongue, though familiar to me. And unlike words in English, it had no accented syllable, which was the way of most Russian words. Every syllable counted. So, for Mr. Nabokov, did the music of words, and he sometimes read us a passage we did not understand for its lilt, for the rhythm and pace of the Russian sentence, and a broad grasp of the way Russian sounded. There were no technical aids or short cuts to the teaching of language then, except linguaphone records which we did not use, and we had to plod along with grammar, declensions, conjugations and the solid business of memorizing vocabulary. If the teacher could not convey the feel of language, learning was a dull business. Our class was too fast-paced and full of variety to be dull. Mr. Nabokov, who talked a lot, was very much at home with words. He spoke the beautifully precise and idiomatic English of the cultivated North European, the kind that once distinguished the upper classes in Russia, and now is only spoken outside England by the Swedes. He carried his own English sentences, especially the descriptive ones, to their destination and then around the corner. His use of language had that faculty—of opening up a new vista quite suddenly when you thought you had seen what you came to see. I found it later in his writing of the period, in the stories he was sending to literary magazines while he taught us beginning Russian. Take this sentence from *Signs and Symbols*: "She presented a naked white countenance to the fault-finding light of spring days," introducing an image and then, unexpectedly, another. This onward-going two-image construction was fascinating to me. The only analogy I have been able to find for it, much later, lies in scenery, not language, and only in Kashmir, where in the width and expanse of the valley, a turn in the road you are travelling can confront you with a vivid new sight.

Mr. Nabokov could, in our teen-age lingo, be "hilarious." "Take the Russian verb 'ostanavlivat,'" he said, "which means 'to stop.' In the days of the horse carriage it was all right to shout 'ostanavlivaite' to a man about to cross the street, to save him from an oncoming vehicle. But in our automobile culture the poor fellow would get run over before the warning was out, so nowadays it is customary to say 'stop.'" Some words, he told us, become international with use, like "bifshtek" or "djaz."

I had entered the class with an advantage. Loving languages, I had started Russian the previous summer with a gifted eccentric teacher who had a nervous breakdown every few years under the strain of teaching fourteen languages. I could already read simple Russian and converse in it. I did not deserve Mr. Nabokov's casual remark to a colleague, conveyed I do not remember how to me, that "Mees Pandit" was the most brilliant and beautiful girl in his class. But I cherished the compliment and became more expansive in class.

I don't know how aware Wellesley was that it sheltered at the time two giant reputations-in-the-making: in the Spanish department, Jorge Guillen, who was to win the Spanish-speaking world's most prestigious literary prize in 1976, and Vladimir Nabokov, who in a few years, with the publication of *Lolita*, would win international acclaim and be able to devote himself exclusively to writing. My 1947 *Yearbook* makes no mention of either and does not even list a Russian department.

I used to meet Senior Guillen in corridors. Did everyone look tall to me because I was young and small? Or was he actually as tall as I remember him, with a humorous gleam in place of a smile, eyes that closed when he talked, books under one arm, bending his head to talk to a colleague or a student? I knew him only at greeting distance. Spanish was taught to me that year by Senorita Oyarzabal, a frail, angular, aristocratic refugee from France's Spain, whose love for her country was overlaid by a bitter nostalgia. I wanted to weep in her class. Such a sadness clung even to Spanish verbs under her guidance. Far from home myself I was acutely conscious of her yearning for her promised land, country of countries, home, Spain, of which all that was left to her now, and perhaps forever, was memory. I understood the Senorita in my bones, and thought of the irony of a world where some dictators were destroyed and others flourished, driving good people from their homes.

I knew Mr. Nabokov was a refugee too, of longer standing than my Spanish teacher. Asides and explanations during the stories we studied in class lit up the life he had left: the huge country estate he had lived on as a boy, complete with footmen and maids, governesses and tutors; the trips to Europe, French culture and English learning lying like lace frills on the surrounding Russian fabric. He did not indulge in continuous recall of this kind. It came out where it was relevant to what we might be reading at the time. He never told us his family had left Russia soon after the Revolution, never to return, and that his father had been assassinated in 1922, the year he took his degree in modern languages from Trinity College, Cambridge. And except that he had travelled a lot, lived in England as a student, in Germany and France and then in America, there was nothing of the homeless wanderer about him, nothing of drama or disaster, no smear of self-pity or anger, not a single suggestion that an entire past had been wiped out behind him.

I knew a Russian émigré family who lived near Wellesley. The Berestneffs were warm-hearted, hospitable extroverts. At Russian Easter the Russian wife of an American foreign correspondent I knew took me to a party at their house. Sixteen then, I had never been to such a party. They ate and drank Russian delicacies, wine and vodka, sang Russian songs to the accompaniment of a balalaika with an emotional extravagance that swept me off my feet. Mr. Berestneff took my hand and charmed me into dancing with him. Yet as the evening wore on a haunting melancholy pervaded the festivity. These were people who had never left Russia, and never would. All else was wilderness and exile. It left an indelible impression on me. This was what being driven from one's own soil did to people. They drifted and pined. The outer framework of their lives, though they might spend the rest of their lives in it, remained outer. Shadows became real, and the real never took firm shape. The troop ship I had come to America on—no passenger ships were crossing torpedoed seas then—had carried 700 Polish refugees, immigrants who had the look of dry shed leaves waiting for another wind. Those had been poor, destitute people, while the Berestneffs were privileged and cultured. But their plight seemed oddly similar, oddly futureless. I had not then met Mr. Nabokov.

When I did, I could not imagine him at the Berestneffs. I don't know if he knew them. There was an intellectual exactitude about him that did not wallow in anything. He was brisk and energetic. He walked miles in that classroom. He had no mannerism we could get hold of, no obvious way of talking or gesticulating, nothing to label "foreign" or quaint that would relegate him to a collector's item among teachers. He had a quick sympathetic smile for atrocious pronunciation, charity for our mistakes, and a kindly interest in our efforts. But he did not spill over onto us. Student-teacher rapport of the sort now considered a necessity was not a violent need or demand in those days. There was a generation gap and there was expected to be one. A society, its ages and stages of life all glued together in a heart-to-heart association would have seemed hideous and preposterous. I don't know if any student had an outside-class, come-to-my-house relationship with Mr. Nabokov. I did not and I don't believe any such existed. Even in class his teaching had a trim and tailored elegance. He did not go into transports, and he did not allow words or ideas to go on a spree. Senorita Oyarzabal got carried away with passages of the Spanish poets. She reminisced while she taught. It was part of the wistful spell she wove. With Mr. Nabokov we remained with the lesson. Yet if we were reading an extract from Pushkin's *Queen of Spades* or lines from a Lermontov poem, we "saw" the scene as he explained it to us in detailed visual miniatures re-creating the vanished setting of Tsarist Russia with its high bourgeoisie, and its hard-drinking, duelling officer class. We saw it as in a mirror, or framed in wood, or glimpsed through an archway, alive and peopled, but confined to its own space and time, not intruding on ours. He filled us in with wit and a clear eye on the background, history or personality we were reading about, but it was *there* and we were *here*, and there was no confusing the two. For the first time I dimly understood—though the understanding did not serve me till later when I began to write—that fact and fiction, "here" and "there," were different, two realms, and for the fastidious artist must always remain so. It may have been this capacity to be so actively in the present himself that made Mr. Nabokov un-refugee-like. An ironic half sentence from his story. "A Forgotten Poet."—"no matter whether the Tsar be called Alexander, Nicholas, or Joe"—succinctly reveals his devastating detachment for what it really was, the sense of history that kept him whole and healthy, both as human being and writer. Another half sentence at the end of "Mademoiselle O" as surely puts all literary detachment in its proper place, at the far end of heartbreak, not something separate and distinct from the aching, feeling process: "I catch myself wondering whether, during the years I knew her, I had not kept utterly missing something in her . . . something, in short, that I could appreciate only after the things and beings that I had most loved in the security of my childhood had been turned to ashes or shot through the heart." Perhaps only the indomitable among writers and men can rebuild in fiction a world irrevocably lost with so clean and uncluttered a vision, and only a handful of the creative can invent, as Nabokov did, a whole new world on the ashes of the old.

By the time I began to read Nabokov, he had made America peculiarly, breath-takingly, his own. I was not surprised that this encounter did not reflect the voice of the immigrant, or the more sophisticated émigré, or echoes of any other lifetime. This was life in its own right, conveyed in language that was nothing if not lyrically, startlingly original. Of all those who have loved English and made it their own,

Nabokov's use of it has seemed to me the most enriching—the result almost of a meeting between two civilizations, rather than an artist and a new medium, or an exile and a foreign tongue.

Surviving the New Monster*

These are times of ferocious battles for identity. Tiny new nations are obsessed with establishing their identities, by slaughter if need be, in former Yugoslavia. A large new unity like Europe is just as obsessed with passing laws to keep its white identity uncontaminated by non-white immigration. And Islamic fundamentalism is another form of assertion. Here we have our secessionists and fundamentalists but they haven't got the better of us yet. In fact all the usual pointers to identity are vanishing. Indians don't stay where they were born any more. They live and work all over the country and the world. Caste, the big bugbear designed to keep one in one's destined place, has lost its punch. Caste groups once called "lower" have moved into positions of political power and economic clout. We can be sure social mobility is a fact now that matrimonial ads—the acid test of how much equality the traffic can bear—sometimes say "caste no barrier." Today it is politics that keeps caste alive. As for the aristocratic or plebeian origin of names, your chowkidar's son is as likely to be called Bunty, Dimpy or Chimpu as your favourite movie star. Far from identity becoming a fiercer, narrower issue, Indians seem to be letting it rip, watching the hard and fast categories dissolve and disappear to make us more and more indistinguishable from one another. It could be we are old hands at not knowing (or caring) precisely who we are, and have long lived with the many-faceted identity known as "Indian."

We even did without a name for a century or more when, like many other Asians and Africans we were classified as "the subject races" in a world carved up by European empires for the benefit of Europe. Officially they called our countries Dutch East Indies, French Indo-China, German East Africa and so on, in strange contrast to regions where the white man chose to settle (after exterminating or ghettoing the people already there) which were allowed to have names of their own, like Australia, Canada and America. India was divided—nearly a hundred years before the partition of 1947—into "British India" and "the native

---

* *The Sunday Observer*, 15-21 August 1993

states." And within British India we were further chopped up into Hindus, Muslims and sundry other identities, neatly labelled and stored in little cubbyholes for imperial convenience. And as ever, in any process involving human beings, the Indians this chapter of our history produced were all sorts. There was the usual bandwagon of flatterers and *chamchas*. There was a genuine admiration for empire with a Biblical "wonder, love and praise" of it from Nirad Chaudhuri who, quite logically, is now an honorary Englishman. And there was Jawaharlal Nehru who devoted half his life to seeing empires off the map. But far from wiping out Indian identity, empire had a tonic effect on it. We learned what it had to teach us. We sharpened our wits and our claims on it. We united against it. The writing now coming out of the former British empire reflects the vigour and variety of this whole experience not necessarily in the themes writers choose, but simply because they or their parents are direct descendants of an era that is still a part of living memory. It is still the mirror—for good or evil—in which we see ourselves reflected. One's history, whether personal or national, is always here to stay, and literature is partly the use we make of it, as we interpret and re-cycle it into the stuff of our stories. When it wears thin, as the experience wears off once it is worked out of the system, it is time to move on. Are we going to move on?

For a time it seemed we could get past our "post-colonial" phase into a scene and a climate set free from its aftermath, now that empires had had their day and the west was no longer The World. We would be our own masters and set our own standards and imagination would reach new heights. But this doesn't look like happening. The west is more formidably than ever The World. It controls finance and industry, commerce and information, and the technology that governs all those. As in the age of empire, nothing is allowed to interfere with the sanctity of profits, but unlike empire—where human beings met, loved and hated, face to face—the new empire of global managers have nothing on their minds but what makes money. And now that the Soviet Union has disintegrated, there is no other philosophy to balance market-mania. There are sovereign countries in place of imperial "possessions" but they have very little say in vital decision-making.

Politically it is a world in which it is all right for George Bush to plot the murder of Saddam Hussain and massacre a few hundred thousand Iraquis in trying to achieve it, but it is not all right for Saddam Hussain to plot the murder of George Bush. Economically it is a world where the capture of forests and minerals and other natural resources will go on order to maintain the lifestyles of the world's richest and most privileged people. Culturally it is a world where Rupert Murdoch will soon be in control of the air waves over Asia, and what he gives us we will watch. And of course it is a world where books, like art and sport, are big business. Hype, promotion and advertising are more important than the book. Will we who came through imperial times proud and whole survive the monster of commercialism? Or are we in for a flood of "marketable" books, pointless exercises in exotica to suit the western and obliging Indian palate? Already it looks as if maharajas, sadhus, the burning ghats and the like are in for a brand new lease of life, and that Indians must remain quaint if they want to interest others in themselves. Maybe the breakthrough to unselfconscious, straightforward Indianness—so far as Indo-Anglian writing is concerned—will be made by the feminists, perhaps by the Dalits, and others who have stark unvarnished stories to tell.

Hindutva: Art Has the Answer*

My neighbour across the road is handsome, well-travelled and rich. He thinks Margaret Thatcher was Britain's greatest leader and his admiration for America's leadership, and its role in world affairs from Viet Nam to the Gulf War, knows no bounds. His other passion is Hindutva. The fist of Uncle Sam, and Hinduism in its new militant incarnation, may look like an odd couple, but it is a trendy combine, as an adventuring church and adventuring capitalism have been in the past. Trade and the Bible, conquest and the Bible, have gone hand-in-hand all over Asia, Africa and Latin America. Europe's whole imperial enterprise was in Churchill's famous words, "the mission of Christendom." And America followed suit with a huge missionary investment in China, along with business concessions, to save the heathen from damnation and at the same time to turn those hundreds of millions of heathens into good customers for American trade and industry. There has probably been no more successful partnership than the one that raked in profits along with souls. A lady sitting next to George Bernard Shaw at a dinner party told him, "With my beauty and your brains, what remarkable children we could have"—which could be said of the twin offspring of "the mission of Christendom."

Any religion that organizes for war, or missionary enterprise, needs money to finance its campaigns and propaganda. America has both the money and the Indo-Americans who have been sold the message that Hindutva is Hinduism. All those bricks for Ayodhya, all the organization it took to get them there, all the videotapes about them, might not have been possible on that scale but for American dollars. And the Vishwa Hindu Parishad, being worldwide, obviously counts on worldwide currency. All public causes need money, but how times have changed! Mahatma Gandhi collected five rupees for his Harijan Fund in return for every autograph he gave. He passed the hat around at his meetings for contributions that ranged from two-anna coins to gold

---

* *The Sunday Observer*, 12-18 September 1993

bangles. He had a patron, too,.Mr. Birla. But not much more was required of Mr. Birla than a room in his house, some fruit, nuts and goat's milk. Even this led Sarojini Naidu to quip, "What it costs the nation to keep the Mahatma in poverty!" Mrs. Naidu would have been speechless today when money is calculated in black, white and crores, hospitality has to be five-star, every petty politician has his sugar daddy, and Hinduism—which Gandhi in his innocence believed meant loving your neighbour—has become a war to recapture the birthplace of someone who may not have been born there at all. He may not, in fact, have been born anywhere, except in the reverence and rapture of his devotees—and what better place to be born!—who need no bricks and mortar to back up their faith. But this possibility has been overlooked by the sadhus, sadhvis and politicians now getting ready for the second round of bricks and mortar.

Gandhi created a non-violent mass movement by counting on the participation of men and women who had hardly a rupee to their names and did not own a change of clothes. In contrast, Hindutva's first attempt at winning mass participation has depended on wealthy patrons and lavish funds. A campaign that cost a fortune ended in a fury of destruction, and its fallout brought death and desolation to thousands of Indians.

The artists, writers, musicians and political activists who gathered at Ayodhya under Sahmat's banner, and staged the exhibition "Ham Sab Ayodhya," made the most heartening news on an otherwise deplorable national scene. Much has been written, even by those who, in principle, supported the Sahmat show, about the poor judgement of the organizers in using a government donation, and secondly, for using texts from a Buddhist scripture that would cause controversy. The criticism about hurting Hindu sentiment need not disturb us. No Hindu has ever been hurt, or even puzzled, that a man believed to be God turned his innocent and pregnant wife out of the palace to give birth alone in the jungle. If Hindus can live with Sita's banishment, suffering and suicide, and still worship the husband responsible for it, then we can live with any outrage on earth, and a Buddhist text won't upset us.

The other two criticisms sound unnecessarily shy and shrinking. If the government makes funds available for a just cause, the power-play behind the donation need not concern us. And those who want to avoid public controversy by confining prickly issues to academic circles are missing the point. Untouchability—a thorny issue—was not tackled by academic debate, but by political action and the rise of a literature that threw the searchlight on such evils. We need more, not less, such exhibitions and concerts as Sahmat put together to keep today's greatest danger—religious fundamentalism—before the public eye. The artist, especially, cannot stay away from commitment and participation at a time when art and the people must join forces to reaffirm the rich and complex heritage of India. The answers to Hindutva cannot come out of learned debate by scholars in seminars. They will come out of a new age of stories, theatre and song. I, for one, hope the Sahmat venture is the first of many, for it would be fatal to retreat and leave the people of India to be manipulated by fanatics.

At the Mercy of Her Izzat*

Up the road from where I live there is a husband who is trying to gain sole possession of the house he shares with his wife. As she insists on living in it, he has confined her—under constant harrassment—to the upper floor, and now attacks and threatens to kill her unless she leaves. The lady's relatives have disapproved of her reporting his behaviour to the police. It is unseemly to make private family matters public. The police ask such awkward questions. So never mind if you are murdered. Down the road, at a crossroad, a girl was raped by three men a few days ago. Neither the police nor the local press were informed because the family feared publicity would bring disgrace on them. Domestic terror and rape are not as important as "izzat." These are, one might say, the hazards connected with being a woman (and therefore a half-person) in what we call normal times, in a country where social attitudes are stuck in the dark ages. Being a woman under a fundamentalist government is a joy Indian women have not yet tasted, although what women have to fear under any form of religious fundamentalism is not guesswork. There is plenty of history, and plenty of current evidence, to go on.

Whether fundamentalism flies the flag of Islam or Hinduism, Christianity or Sikhism, women are its first victims. Unfortunately the forces that act as chains on women are those of religion and tradition. High priests know no other laws, and it is they who decide what people may read or write, what constitutes a crime and how the guilty shall be punished. The latest example we have is of a Bangladeshi writer, Taslima Nasreen, a champion of women's rights, who has infuriated the mullahs by her novel *Lajja*, and has been sentenced to death by a fundamentalist group. And though this fatwa does not have government sanction, the government has not spoken out or taken action against it. What the high priests of any fundamentalist creed require of women is no different from the "Kitchen, church and kindergarten" credo Hitler laid down for the Nazi female model. Man is master, and women are

---

* *The Sunday Observer*, 17-23 October 1993

obedient daughters, docile wives and good breeders. A Sadhvi Rithambara or an Uma Bharati, breathing fire and aggression, and spitting venom, are welcome if they are agents of the fundamentalist cause.

Most communities in India are bound by fundamentalist attitudes, though we have not yet come under a fundamentalist regime. We have burned women as *satis* and we burn them for dowry. We kill them as infants and abort them as foetuses. We leave them undernourished, uneducated and unloved so that there is more food, money and succour for their brothers. The disadvantages most Indian women labour under are so many and so various that the last thing they need is a theocracy that will make all these official, not by law or fiat, but by suppressing the growth and radical reform women are achieving inch by inch by their own efforts. It needs very little to erode this climate and set us back a hundred years. A *sati* could not have been burned in Rajasthan six years ago, watched by an avid audience, if the time had not been judged ripe for feudal and reactionary forces to emerge. Nor could the Shankaracharya of Puri have remarked, as was reported, that two courses were open to widows—suicide or lifelong chastity. But all this, and more, will quietly become part of the body politic if religion comes to power.

Here in the "Hindu heartland" where I live there is to be a state assembly election in December and people tell me there is going to be a Hindu victory. I would be just as apprehensive if the victory were to be Christian, Muslim or Sikh. I do not believe religion and politics make a good mix. Sikh and Muslim separatists have already blown thousands of fellow Indians to shreds, and the proponents of Hindu Rashtra have shown us what the commercialization and vulgarization of religion can do to exploit the gullibility of simple people, and to reduce the giant enterprise of Hinduism to pygmy proportions. Politics brings out the worst in religion. It always has, in every country, and India, if it succumbs, will be no exception. As far as I am concerned there is something repellant about a religion in the race for power, hungry for its spoils, greedy for its rewards. There used to be a song: "I don't want her/you can have her/she's too fat for me." A religion itching for the fat of power is too fat for me. I prefer my religion lean and ascetic and hungry only for God.

In the general disillusionment with political parties, does it matter which party comes to power? Is fundamentalism a phase we have to plough through before we can leave it behind? In a country where a man known as Mahatma consulted his conscience, but not his wife, when he took his unilateral decision to renounce sexual relations with her; in a country where our *netas* who have fathered seven, eight and nine children, probably never consulted either their wives or their conscience before plunging their partners into pregnancies, can fundamentalist behaviour be more damaging to the concept of women as human beings with minds and bodies of their own? The answer to that is yes, things can be worse, for under a regime of fundamentalism we will be up against the blank wall of ideology, not the more changeable stuff of social habit and individual temperament. We will then go by the Book, the prophet, and the priest, and if you argue with any of those you face the firing squad, as Taslima Nasreen is doing. So it is of some importance that women do not help to bring religion-based parties to power. Indian women have too much to lose.

In Varanasi last year I asked a college principal whether women took part in the city's social life. She emphatically said they did. They regularly visited temples, and observed the feasts and fasts. If this is life, I thought, can death be far behind?

Delhi: Body but No Soul*

Those who have roots in Delhi claim that Delhi has a soul. It is the site of buried cities, seat of empires, and now the capital of a republic. The city certainly has a history. But who hasn't? History is only a matter of time. Life and soul are something else. The great ancient cities of the world that continue to live and thrive in their modern incarnations have much more than history to their credit. They have met the requirements of a new era and grown another fascinating layer of personality without sacrificing what matters of the past, from architecture to the needs of the human spirit. Delhi, in contrast, strikes me as being in an advanced state of material and spiritual decay.

These may be strong words to describe the capital of what once was, for many years after independence, a great nation, both in achievement and aspiration. But unfortunately I am describing a nation no longer great, and one that has no will to greatness. Everything about Delhi today shows its feeble will, its sagging morale, and its incapacity to get down to businesslike measures that would reverse this condition and inject some hope of change into its own and the country's life.

Delhi must be every town planner's worst nightmare come true. A jungle on wheels clogs the roads and disregards the rules of the road. The thick black fumes of vehicular and other pollution clog the air. It is probably very dangerous to take a deep breath in Delhi. There may still be some priviliged clear air zones but they won't last. The majority of people are lucky if they don't develop throat and lung diseases. Environmentalists who should be at work on a wartime basis on how to clear the air are probably too busy presenting learned papers on pollution at conferences in Paris and Vienna.

Jutting out of this polluted fog are grim grey multi-storey eyesores that make most jail barracks look like the Garden of Eden. The imagination reels at the thought of families actually living in these concrete traps, in broiling summer temperatures and conditions where the

---

* *The Sunday Observer*, 14-20 November 1993

water and power supply keep failing. There is a garden or two in Delhi that still blooms bravely, but I wonder for how long. And of course there is the five-star culture to provide us at astronomical prices with French onion soup and chocolate mousse that we can make better in our own kitchens. I suppose these hotels make money or they wouldn't be there, but on the two occasions I have been taken to lunch at the Meridien's French restaurant, only one other table has been occupied.

When I was in Delhi in October I was asked by a friend to come to a seminar he was conducting on the criminalization of politics. It was an important and timely subject, said my friend, who is an intelligent and concerned citizen. It is timely all right, and has been for at least twenty years. It may well be timely twenty years hence, since no one will have got down to brass tacks about hounding criminals out of politics. Like the filth and pollution, the lawlessness and disorder, it is one of those hardy perennials. I can always go to the next seminar on it if I miss this one, I thought, and so I did not go.

But this theoretical state of affairs is not confined to Delhi, though I am told that the further south you go, the cleaner, more practical and efficient you find Indians. Yet one trend seems to have engulfed us all. Open the colour section of any newspaper and you wonder where you are, and which Never Never Land of fashions, foods and price tags they are catering to. Macdonalds will soon be here, we are informed, but why am I supposed to rejoice that I will be able to eat a tasteless rubbery hamburger instead of the delicious one, flavoured with *hari mirch* and *hara dhania* that I can eat at home? There is something positively demented about the way the media is plunging headlong westward, whether it is a question of what kind of clothes we wear, or if we should go nude. By all means let us kiss and hold hands in public, on and off the cinema screen, stay nude or clothed, sex-smitten or not, if that is the way our own instincts move us, but not because some retarded adolescent in the West is doing it. As discriminating inheritors of one of the world's most sophisticated cultures, why should we become silly imitations of any trend on earth? There is huge scope in India for freeing sex from its shackles, and bringing sex matters out into the open, but the West—a dismal failure in understanding what makes the human spirit tick—is the very last place we should go to for inspiration. No society so caught in the clutches of advertising and the sale of consumer goods as the West is can have the time or interest to cultivate the things that take longer to grow. The cultivation of human relationships, particularly, takes time. But it is westward we are rushing.

Nothing so sickeningly demonstrates our decline as the fact that Delhi counts for zero on the world stage. And nothing has made this so clear as the statement by an advisor to President Clinton that America views "Kashmir as a disputed territory." This piece of ignorance and insolence, surrounded by a well orchestrated accompaniment, including the release of a so-called well researched book that suggests the Instrument of Accession to India could be fake, are no better than we should expect from the co-patriots of Nixon and Kissinger, who gave us a taste of gun-boat diplomacy in the Bay of Bengal, while they wet-nursed Pakistan through the breakup it brought on itself, but there is no reason for this, or any Indian government, to put up with it. It would be quite wrong of us to believe that being economically at a disadvantage, we have no clout. What we do not have is the man or woman this moment of history needs, to tell the world that Kashmir is India's affair and India's affairs will be run by India.

Sins of the Assassin*

So Gopal Godse, brother of Mahatma Gandhi's assassin, has written a book. It is not often that the public gets a look into the heart and mind of an assistant to a violent crime, and one who, in this case, served a life sentence of fourteen years for it, so this will be a rare publishing event.

Jail can be a chastening and transforming experience. Aurobindo received enlightenment in his prison cell, gave up the politics of the bomb, retired to an ashram and devoted himself to his spirit's salvation. Nehru wrote his books in jail, and along with thousands of others he looked upon his repeated incarcerations as pilgrimages on the road to freedom. On that long hard road, men of Gopal Godse's thinking were conspicuous by their absence. They were nowhere to be seen when nationalists boycotted British goods in favour of *swadeshi*; when they fell, or died as Lala Lajpat Rai did, under lathi blows; when in 1929 they took the pledge of independence or in 1942 when the Quit India agitation was launched.

Men like Godse crawled into view, like vermin out of cracks, when it was all over, when the national flag had been hoisted on the Red Fort, and India—albeit partitioned—took her place among the sovereign nations of the world. So ignorant were they in their safe dark hiding places of events in the country that they thought Mahatma Gandhi was responsible for the partition. So consumed were they with hate for their fellow men that they sentenced Gandhi to death for this, and for urging the new Government of India to transfer fifty-five crore rupees to Pakistan. So twisted were their priorities that they who had lifted not a finger against British occupation after the early terrorist phase, made the Indian government their sworn enemy and independence an occasion for mourning. In this lopsided scenario their first act was to kill the man who had inspired and led the world's uniquest fight for freedom, one that had earned the world's respect and admiration. Of the greatest Indian of his generation, the greatest living scientist, Albert Einstein, had

---

* *The Sunday Observer*, date misplaced.

written: "Generations to come, it may be, will scarce believe that such a one as this ever in flesh and blood walked upon this earth." The bullets of Nathuram Godse, ably assisted by his brother, halted those footsteps in their tracks, and nearly forty-six years later, Gopal Godse is proud of the deed, and says he would do it all over again. The book he has written is supposed to let us in on his part of the story. It should also give us a look into the psychology of a fanatic.

It is always a relief when evil comes out of hiding and shows its face, whether in the pages of a book, a press conference, a manifesto, or as happened on December 6th last year, in the demolition of the Babri Masjid. At least we can see and recognize it. But for this forthcoming book, how would we know that a frame of mind like Godse's—apart from his curious agenda for India—is alive and well? The ideologues of this school have been careful on the whole—except for the rabble rousers—to couch their feelings and agenda in affable, somewhat reasonable language. So let's be grateful for this publishing event.

I doubt if I could take such a matter-of-fact view of Godse, his publisher, and his book if India were in danger of an avalanche of Hindu fundamentalism, and we of the secular breed and of the minorities were running for our lives. But so far we live in an India where people like Godse are still an aberration. It is true that events in the past year have made us less confident of our immunity to fundamentalism. A number of learned analyses of Indian identity, and Hinduism, have appeared, which would never have been written if their writers did not perceive a threat to India as we know it. But the importance of a threat can be bloated out of all proportion by the weight of words spent on explaining and analyzing it. Hindutva must be seen in perspective, as a grove of trees in a multifarious forest. Attacking it, or jumping on its bandwagon, may both be over-reactions to what is, after all, a pimple on the landscape, an outburst that has no rationale, no real roots, and therefore no future, for the simple reason that Hindutva is not Hinduism. The religion and culture that have nourished and sustained us for centuries were there long before this upstart Hindutva sprang up on the scene, and will be there long after it has vanished. What could make the difference between them clearer than that a torch-bearer for Hindutva murdered the saintliest Hindu of our time and delighted in the deed?

The difference seems clear enough to ordinary voters. In Uttar Pradesh where the building of a Ram mandir was the prestige issue, the electorate has voted in an alliance that has vowed to fight communalism and uphold secular democracy. Kanshi Ram, a partner in the alliance, in fact declared that his priority was neither a mandir nor a masjid, but latrines. Though the alliance did not win an absolute majority, its first position is an achievement in a state where no stone was left unturned to whip up Hindutva frenzy.

We will soon see whether Delhi state is going to be governed by a party professing Hinduism or Hindutva. The new government's priorities will depend upon the choice it makes between the two. An enlightened Hindu government will promote an era of religious tolerance and joint religious endeavour. It will turn its attention to the needy and deprived. It will treat Delhi's horrendous problems of traffic control, crime and pollution as urgent priorities. A Hindutva government will probably start digging up the Red Fort and the Purana Quila to build temples on their foundations, and get busy writing its very own version of Indian history. Upon its choice of agenda will depend its vote count the next time around. And as every political party in India has learned, the next time round is no cakewalk.